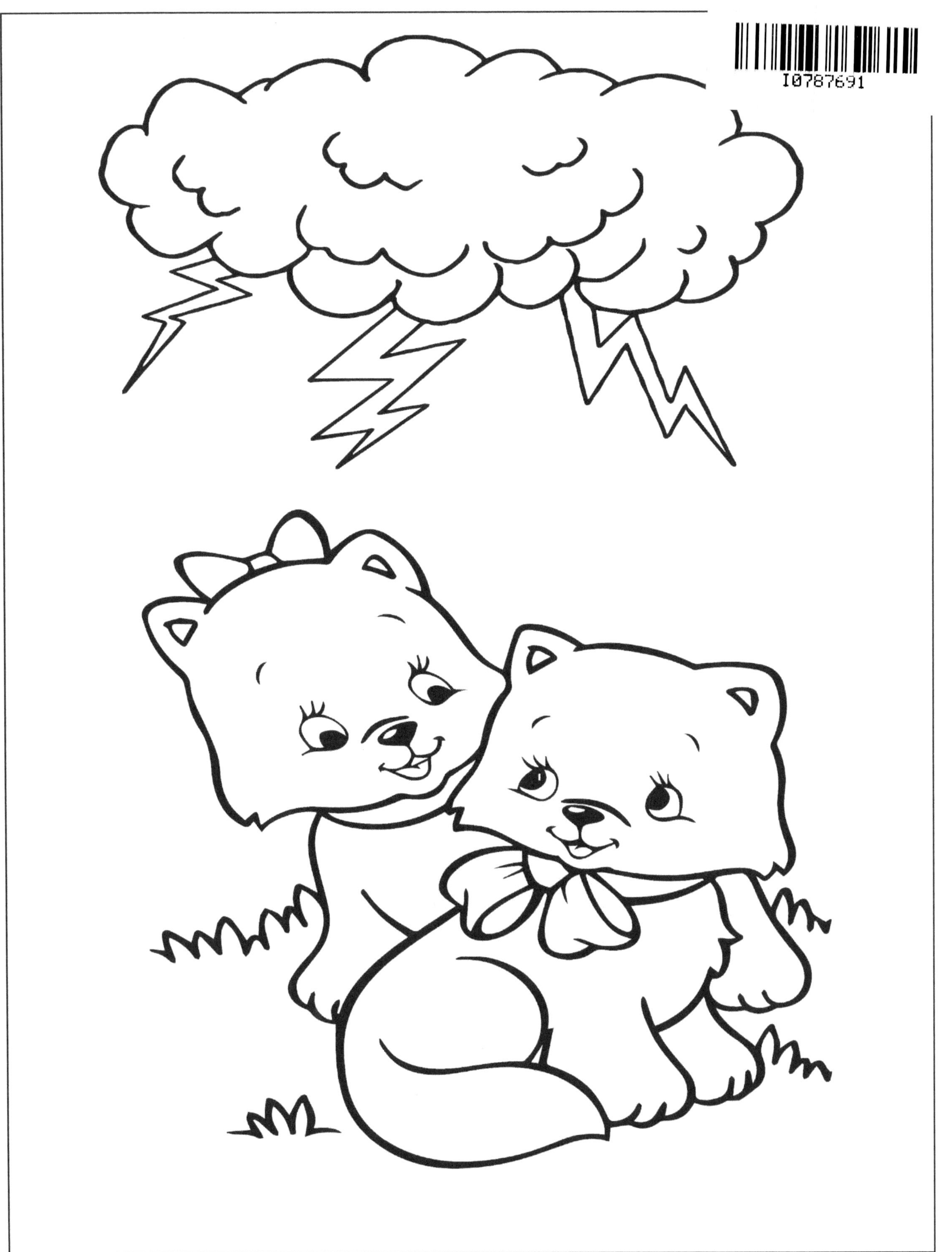

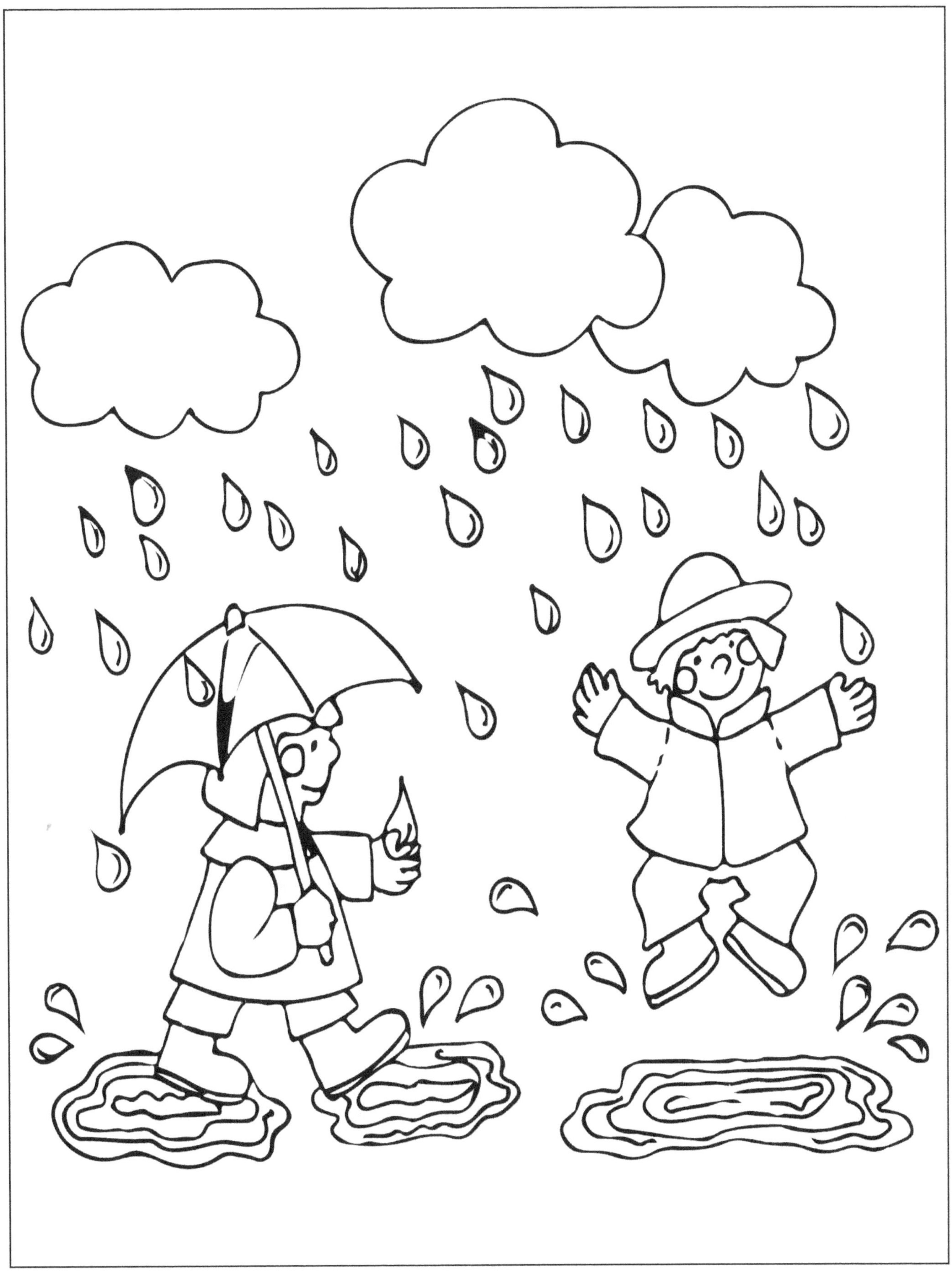

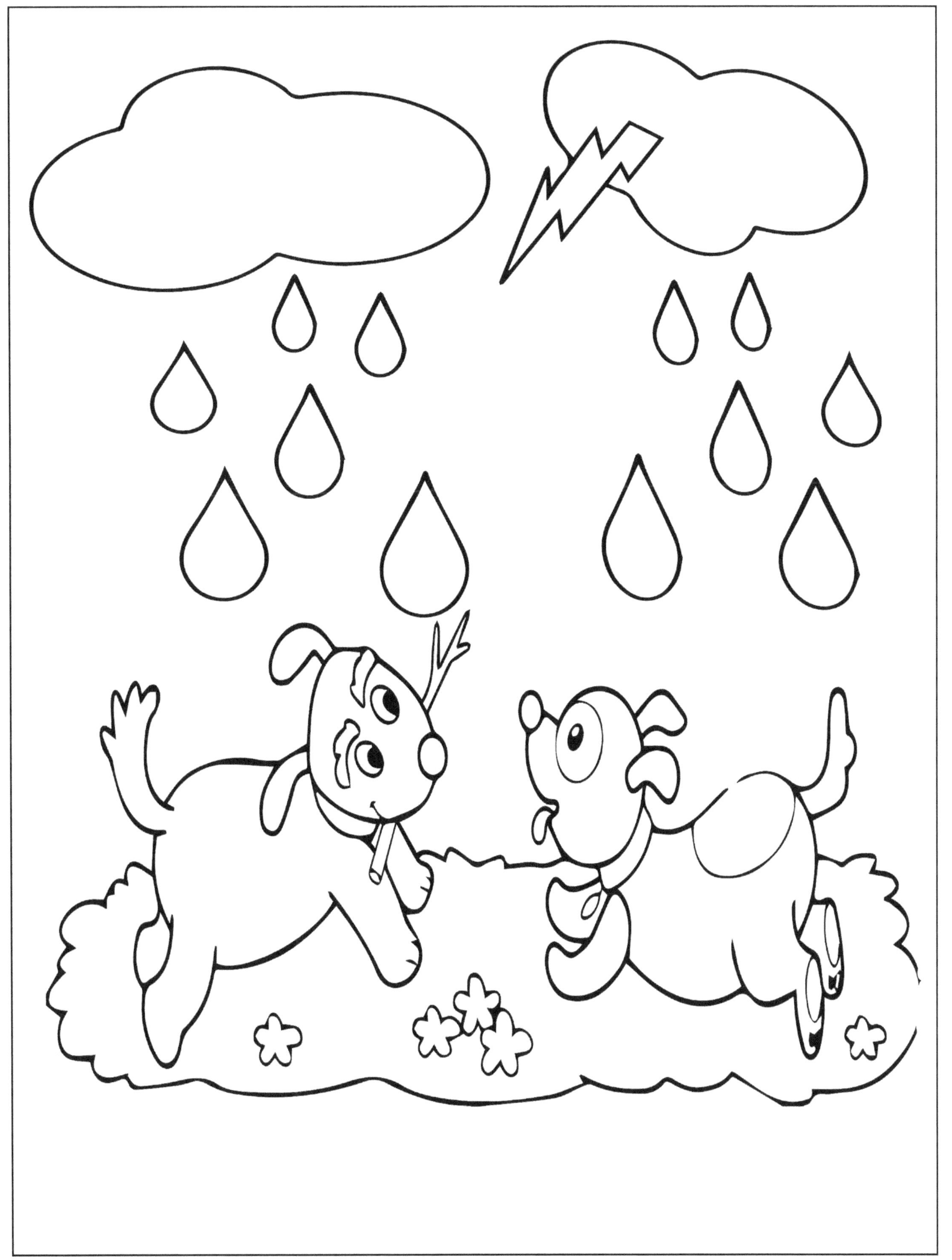

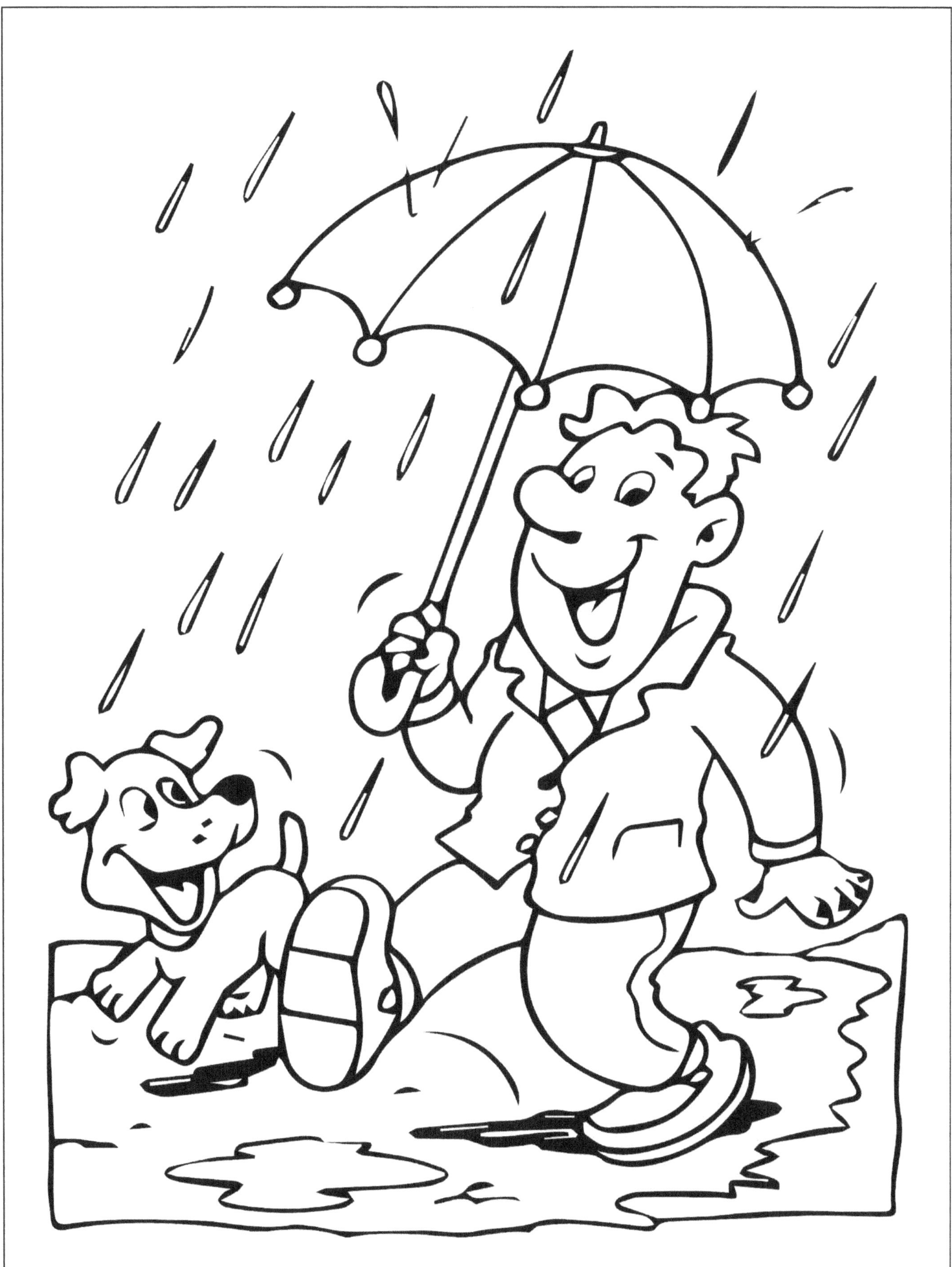

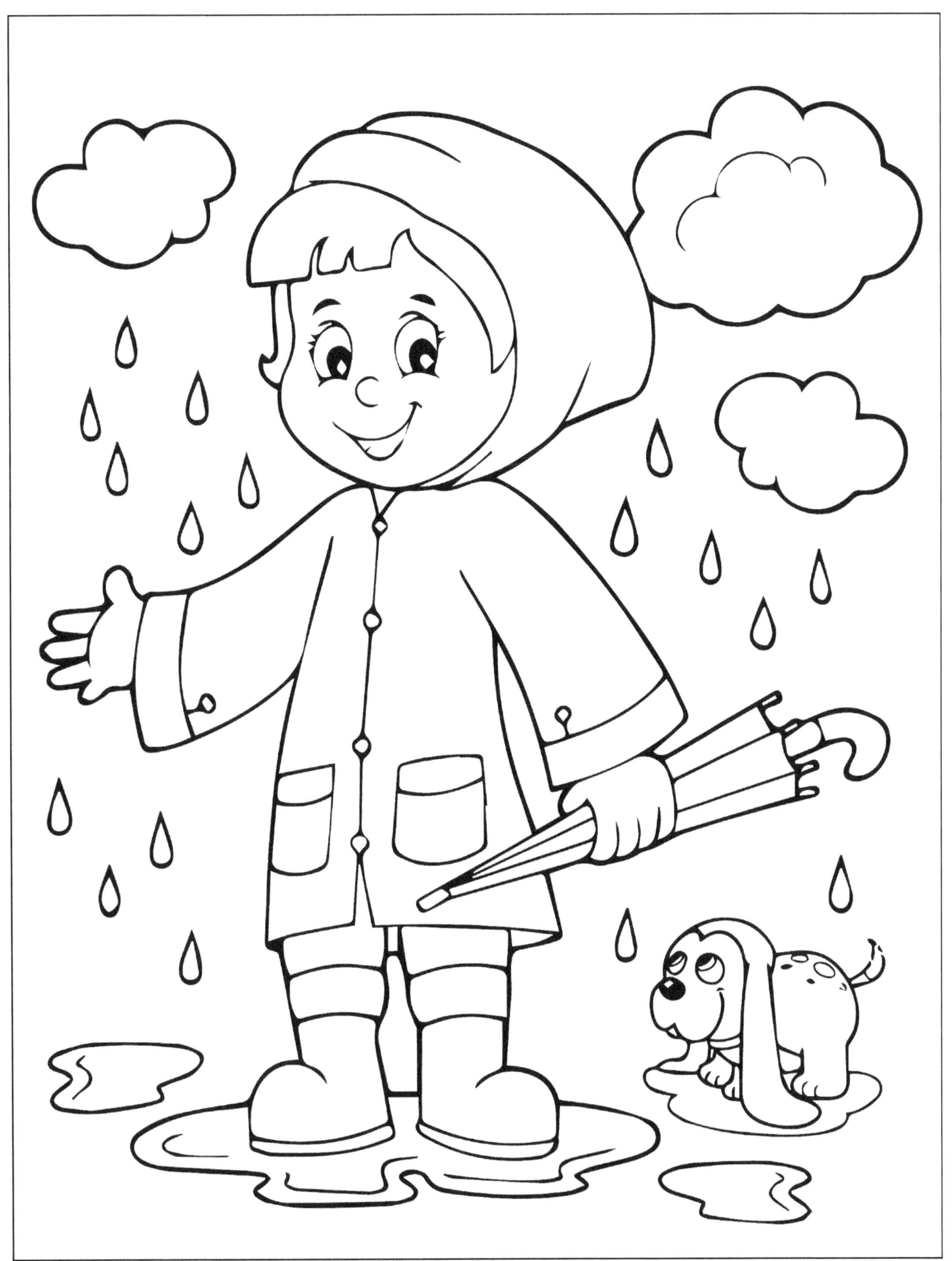

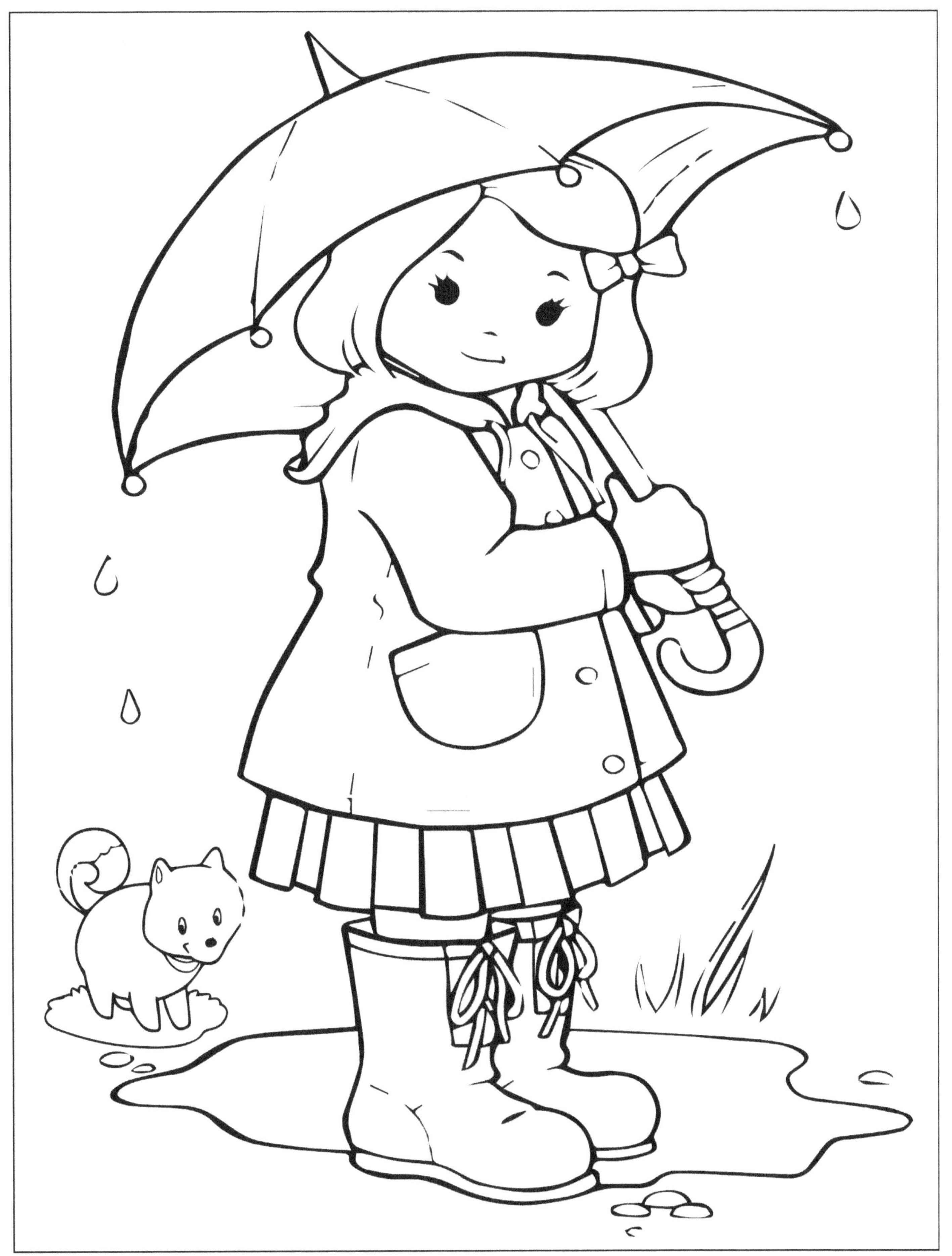

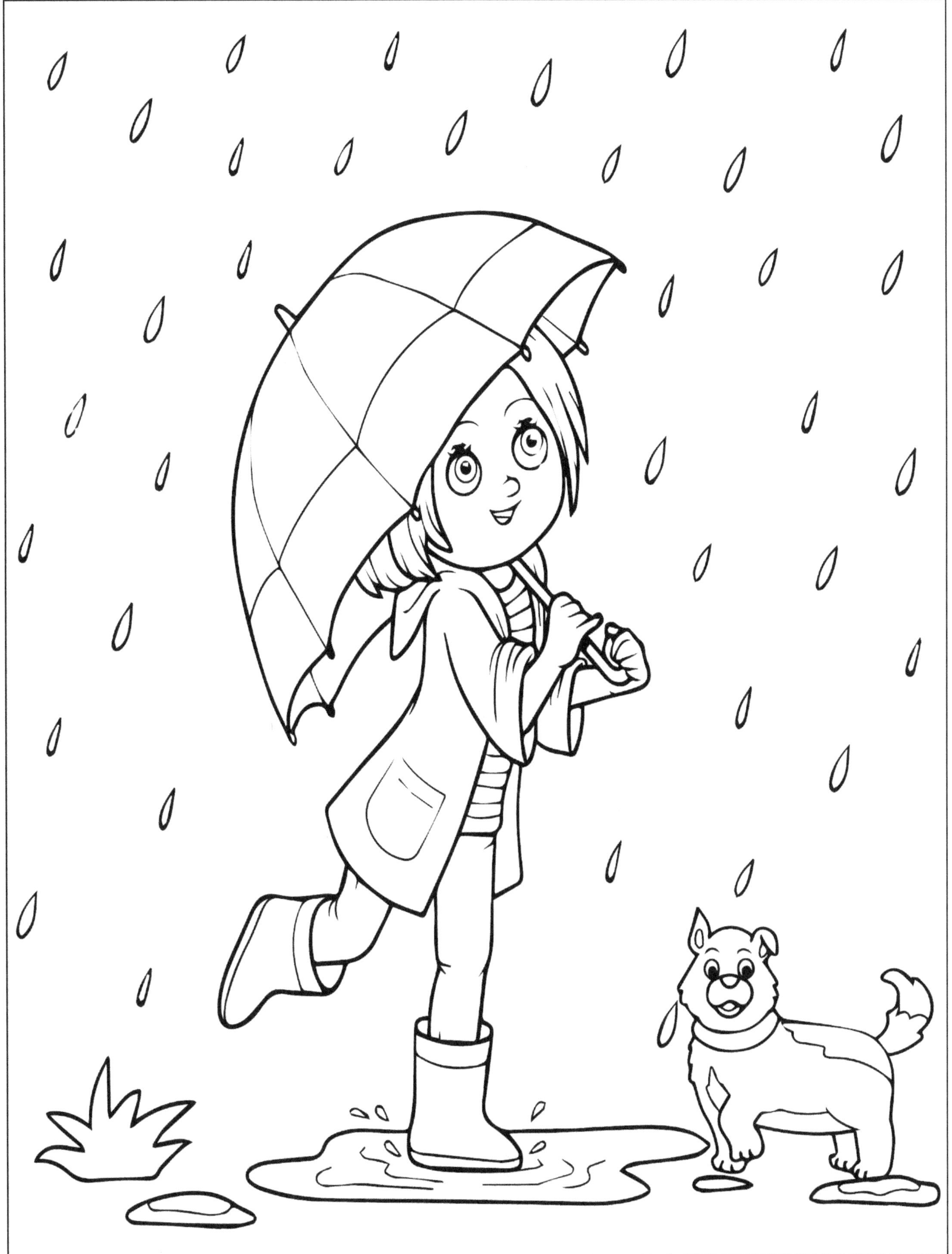

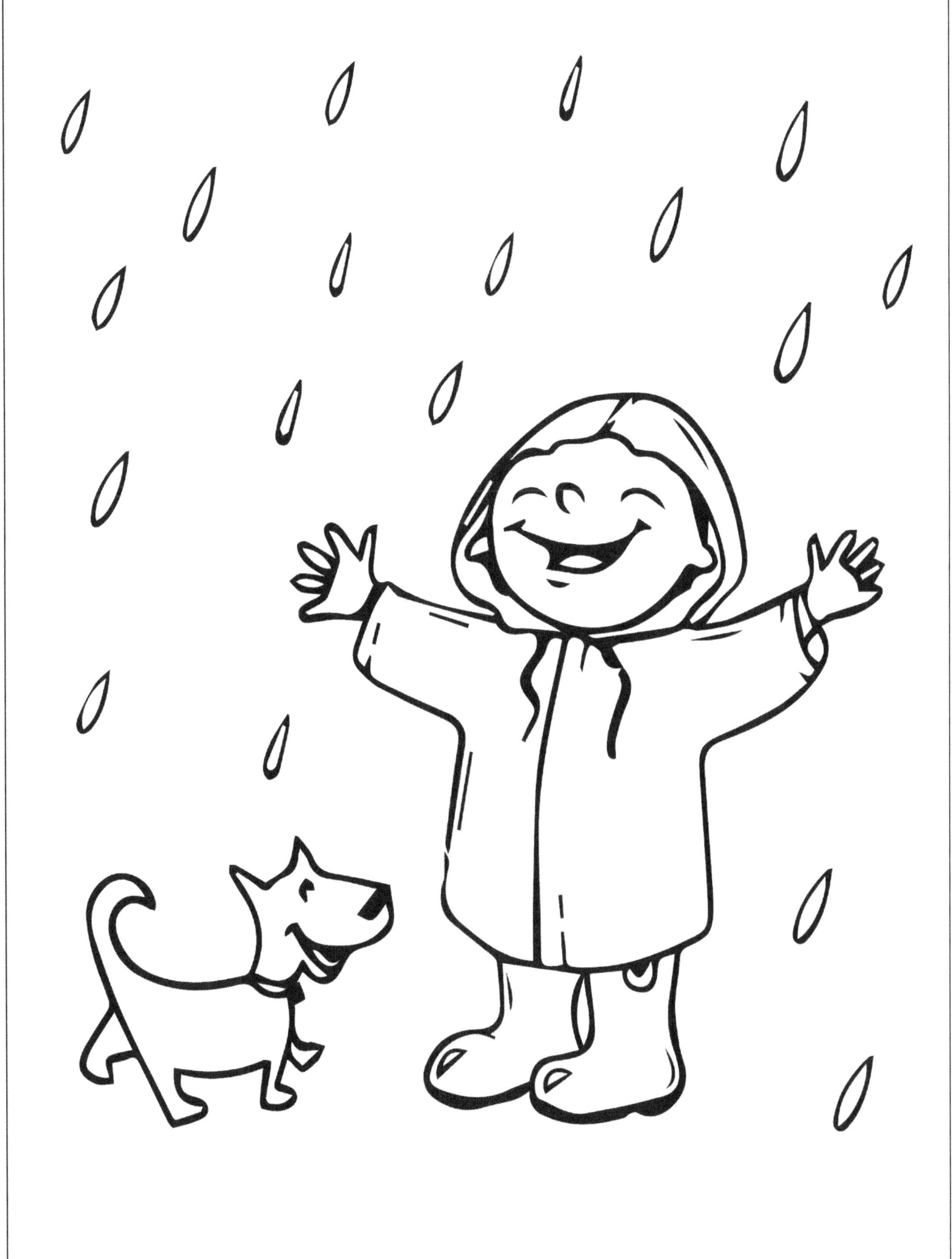

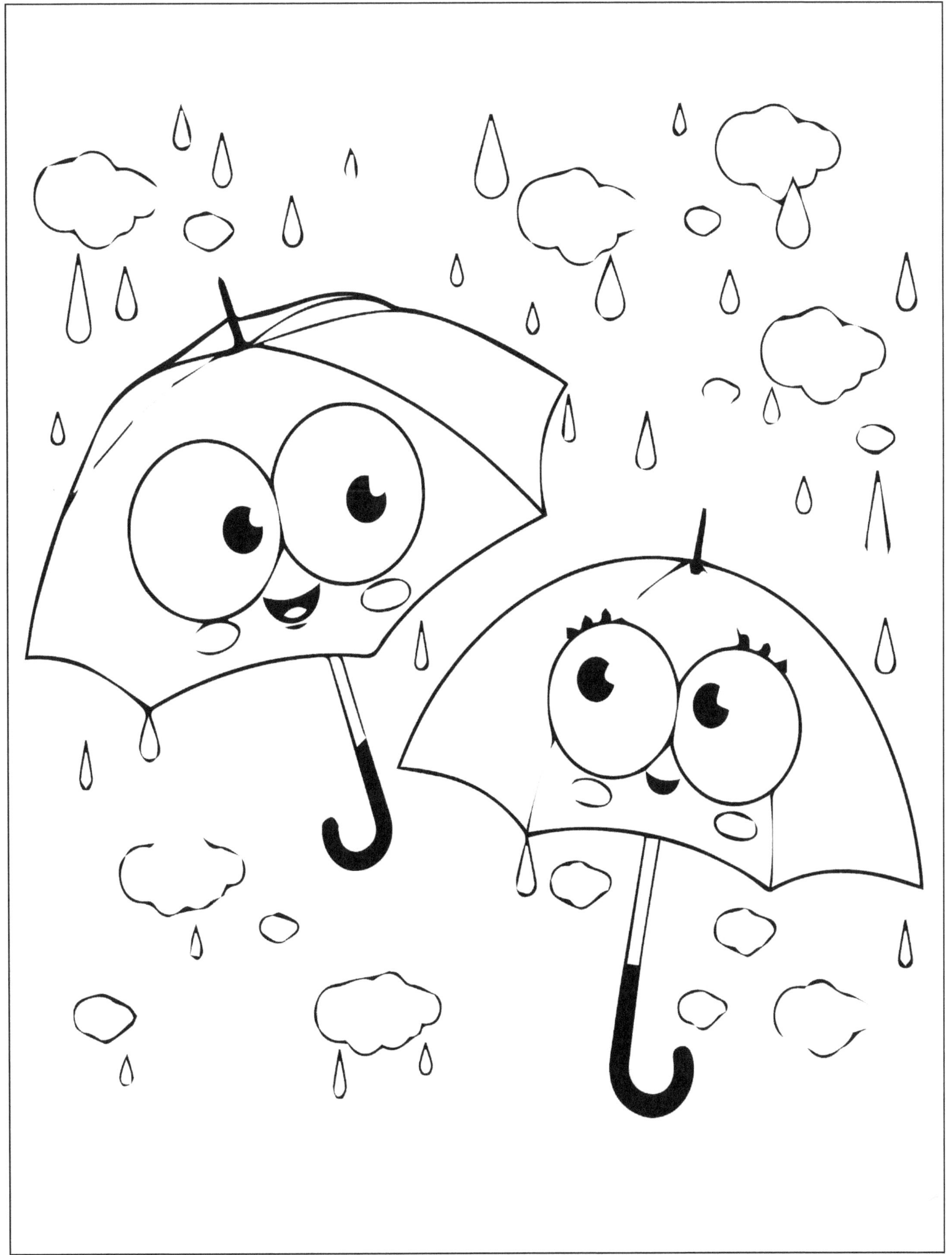

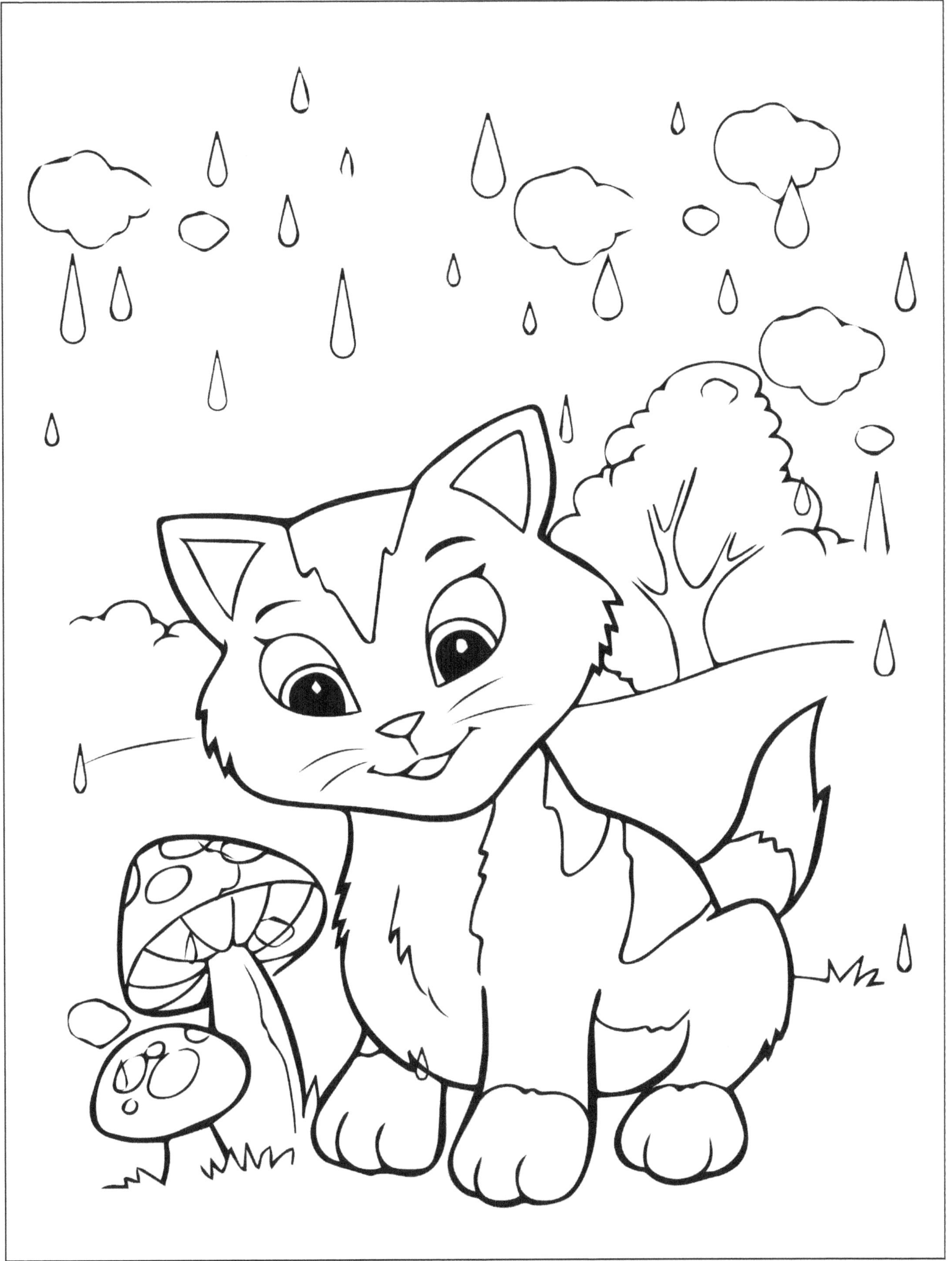

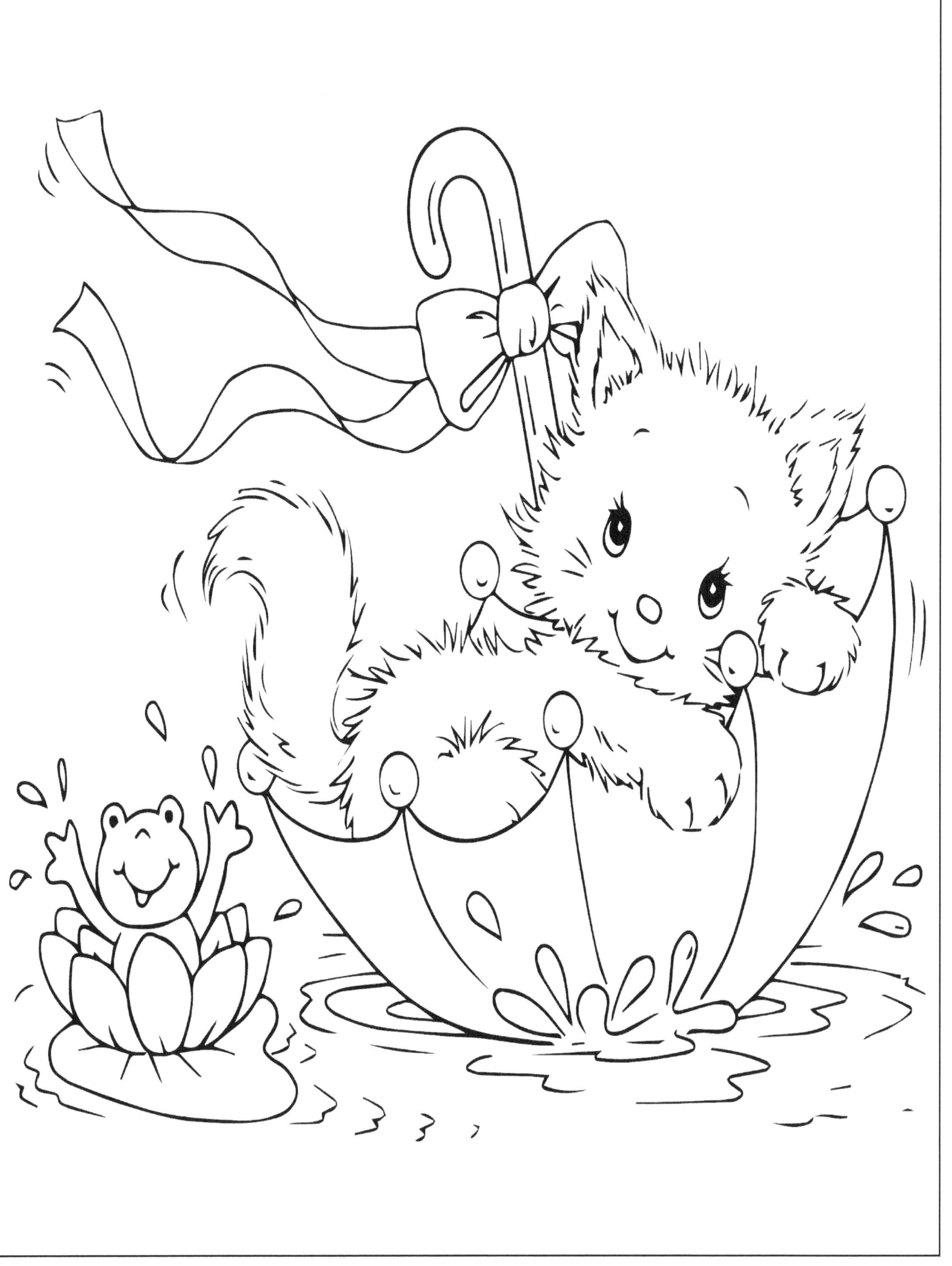

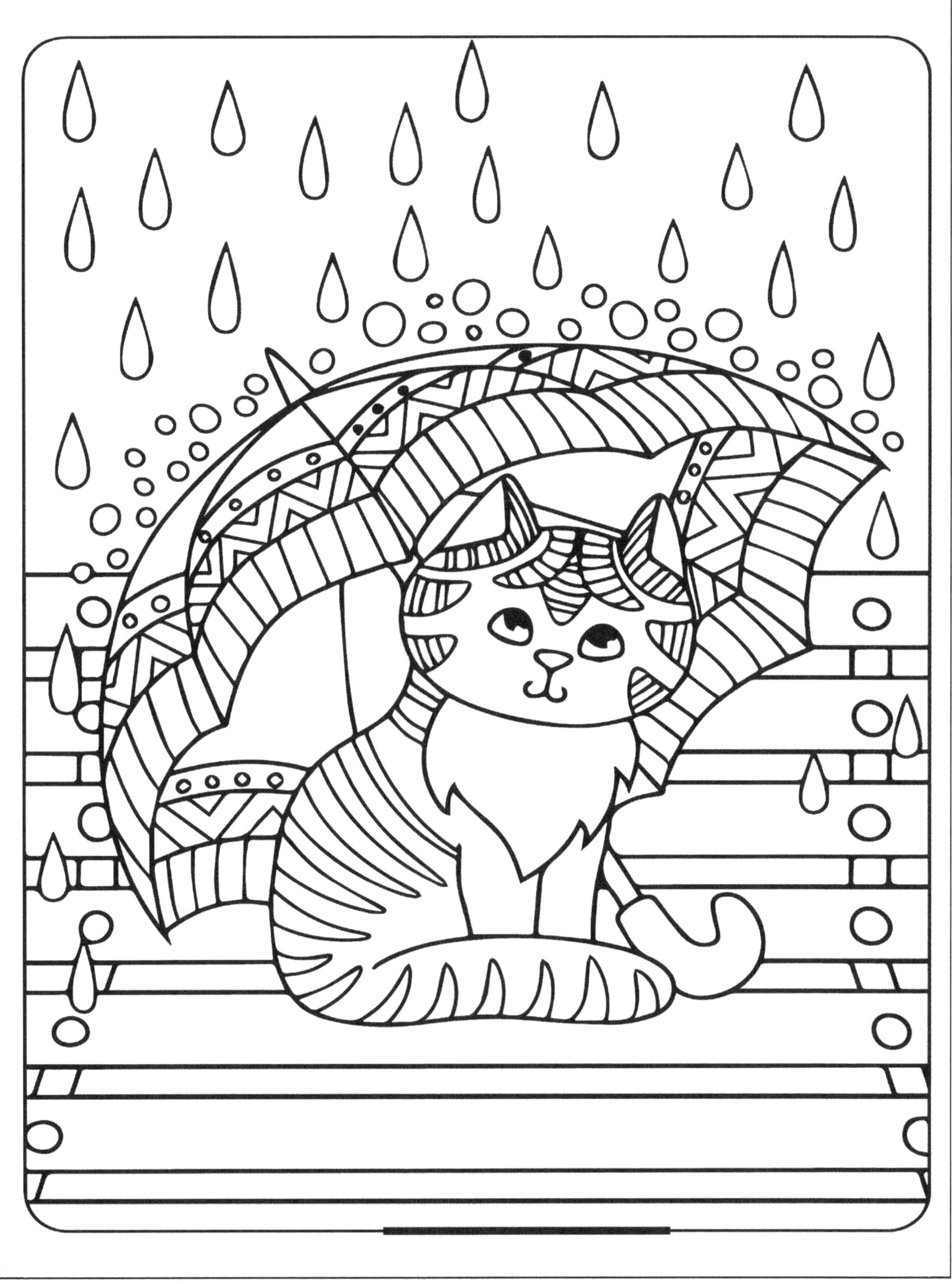

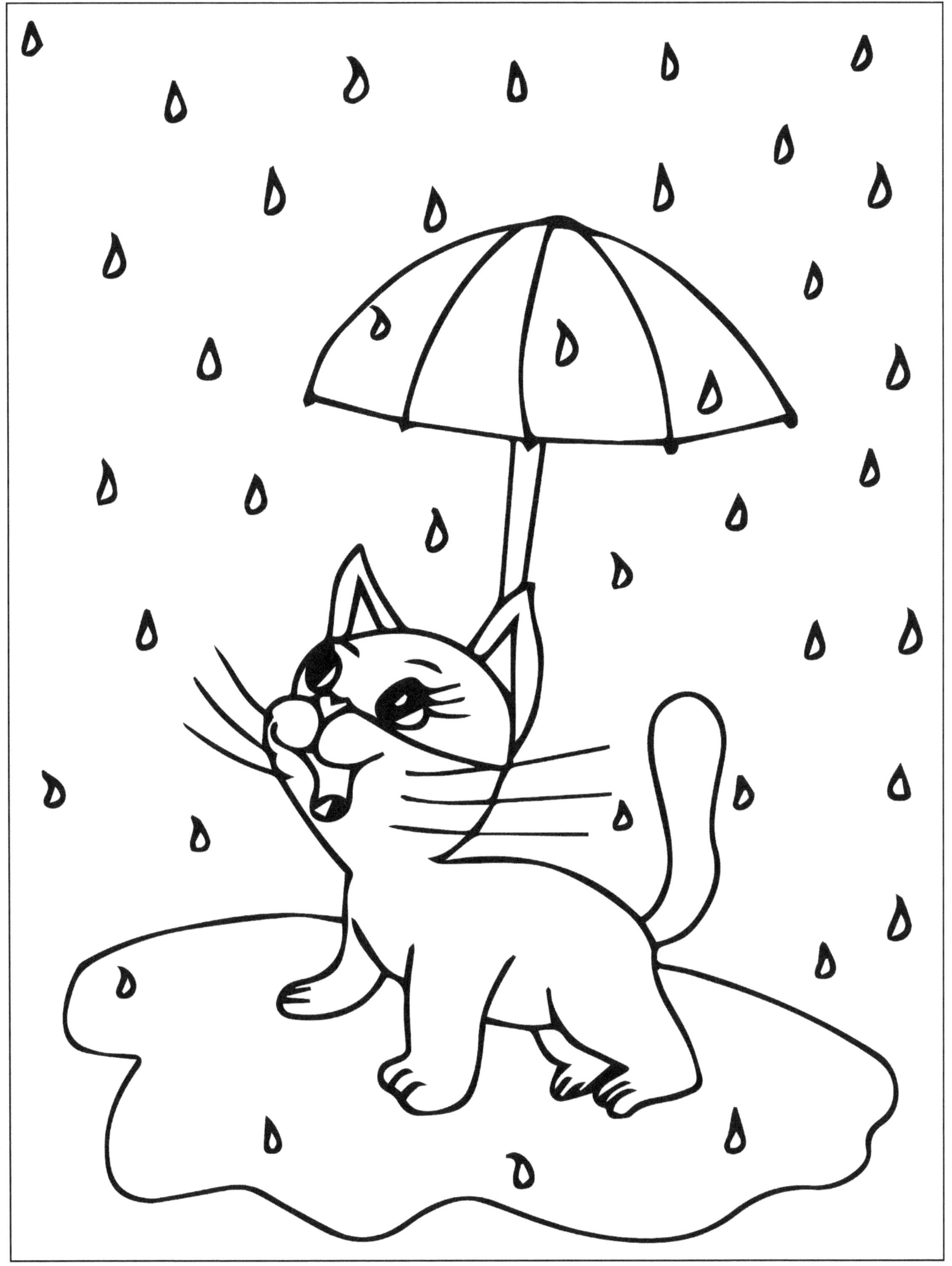

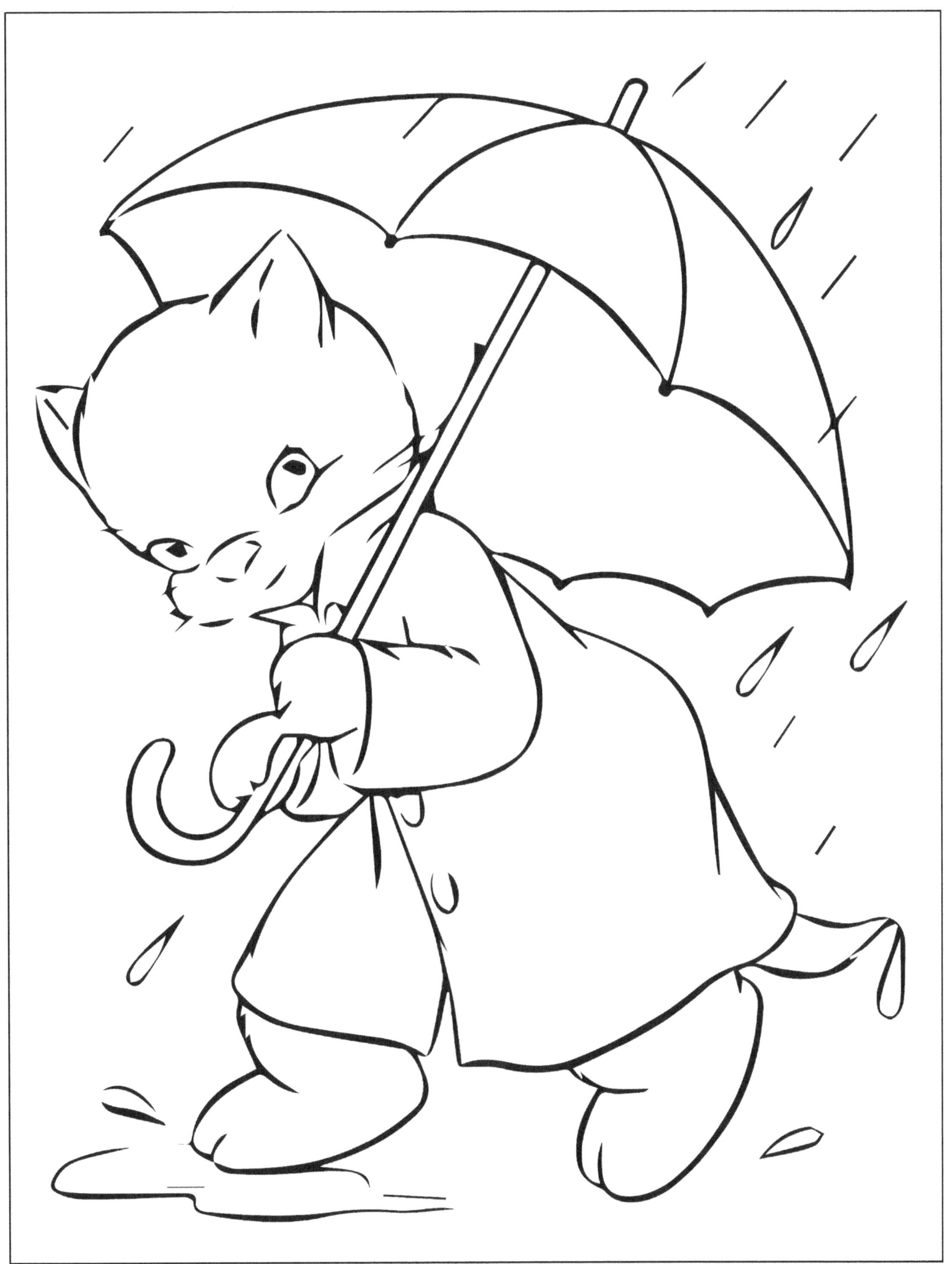

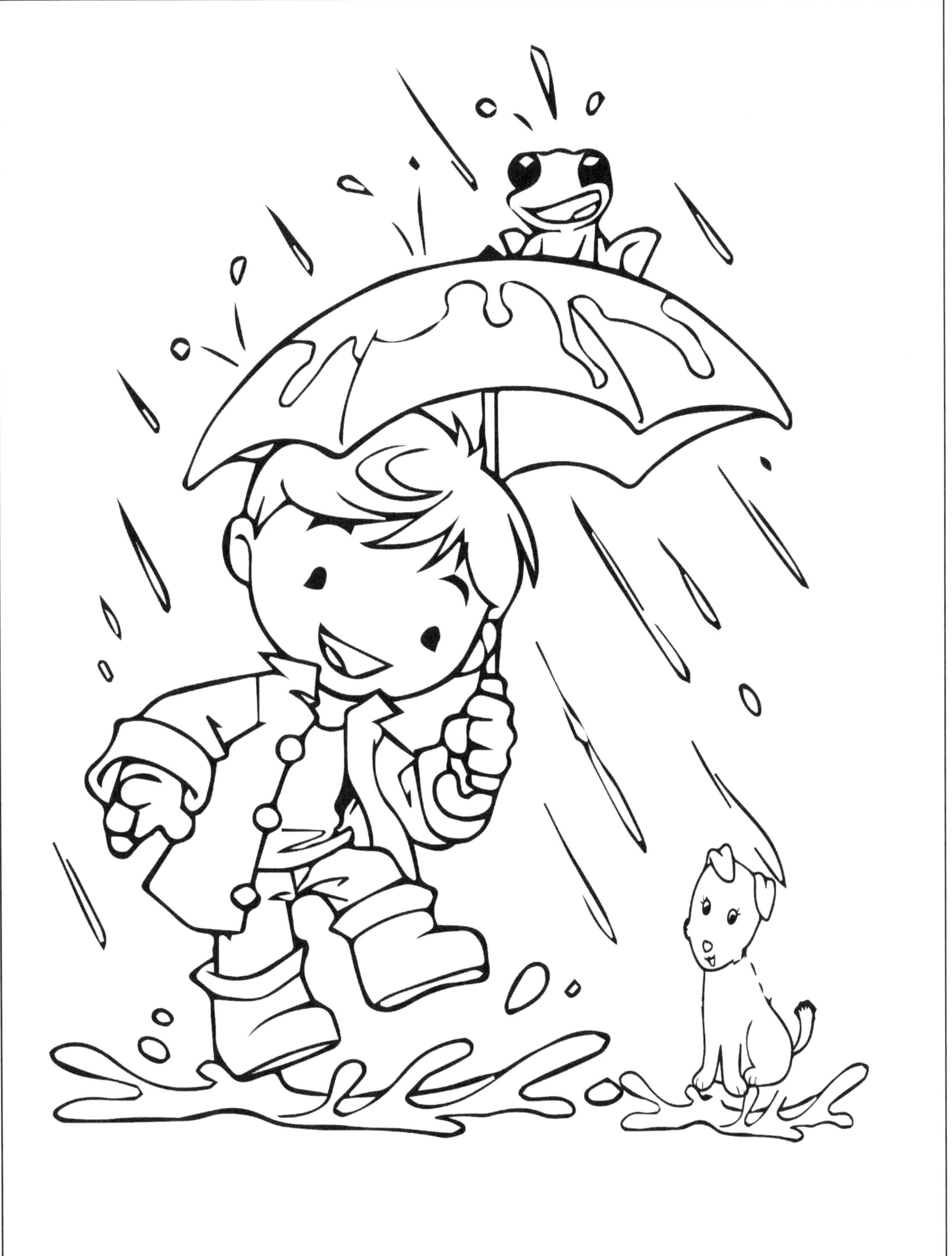

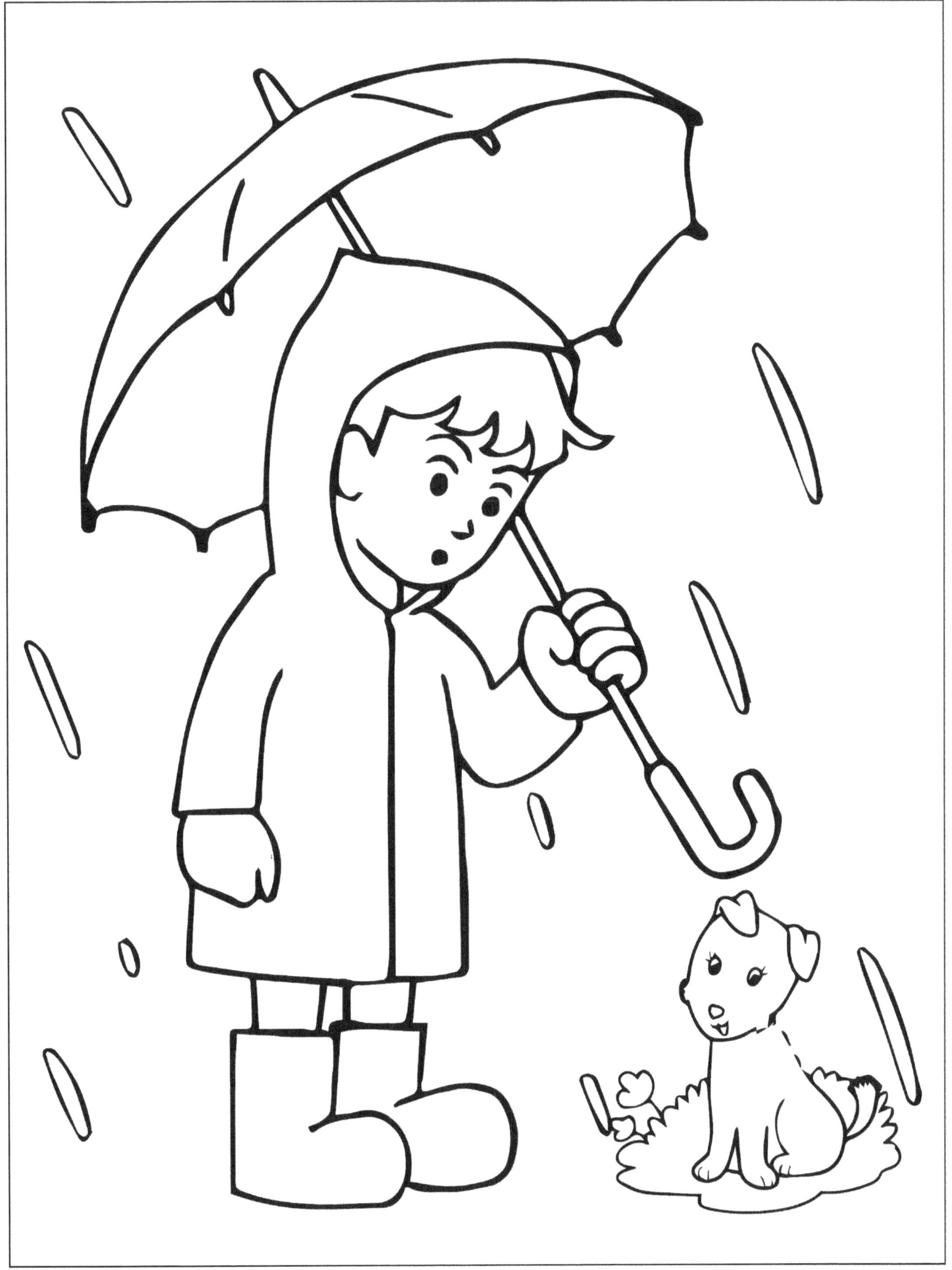

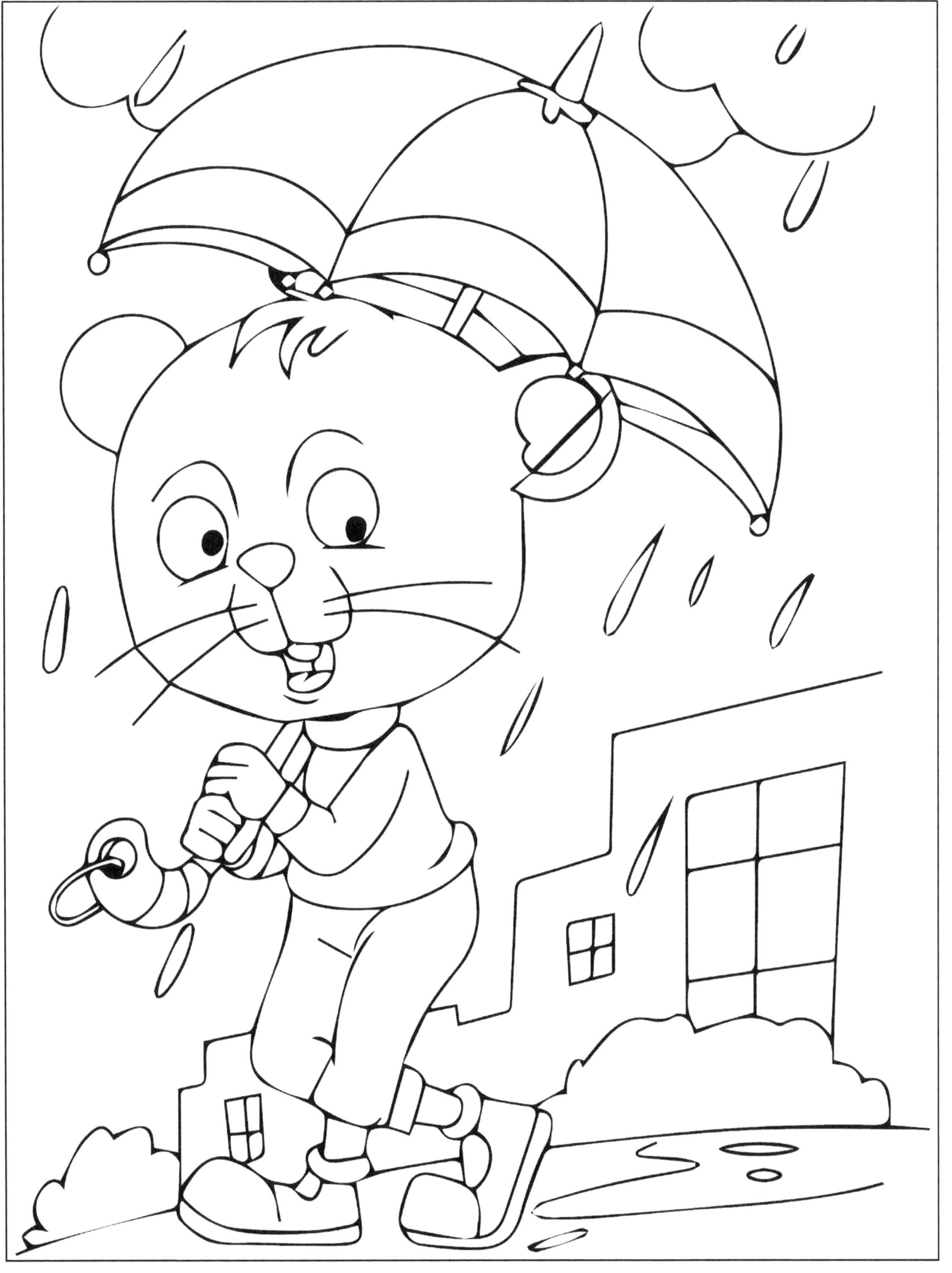

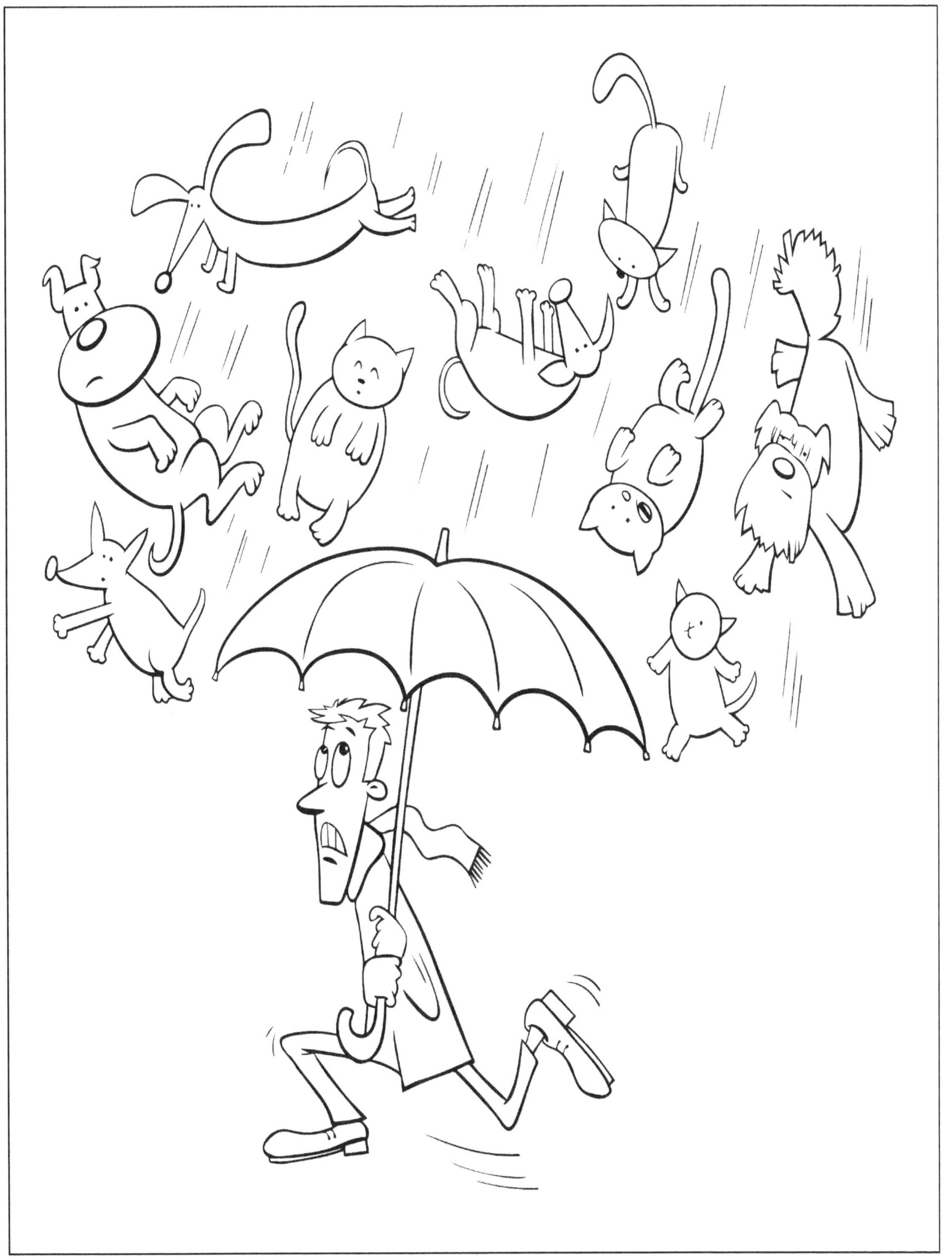

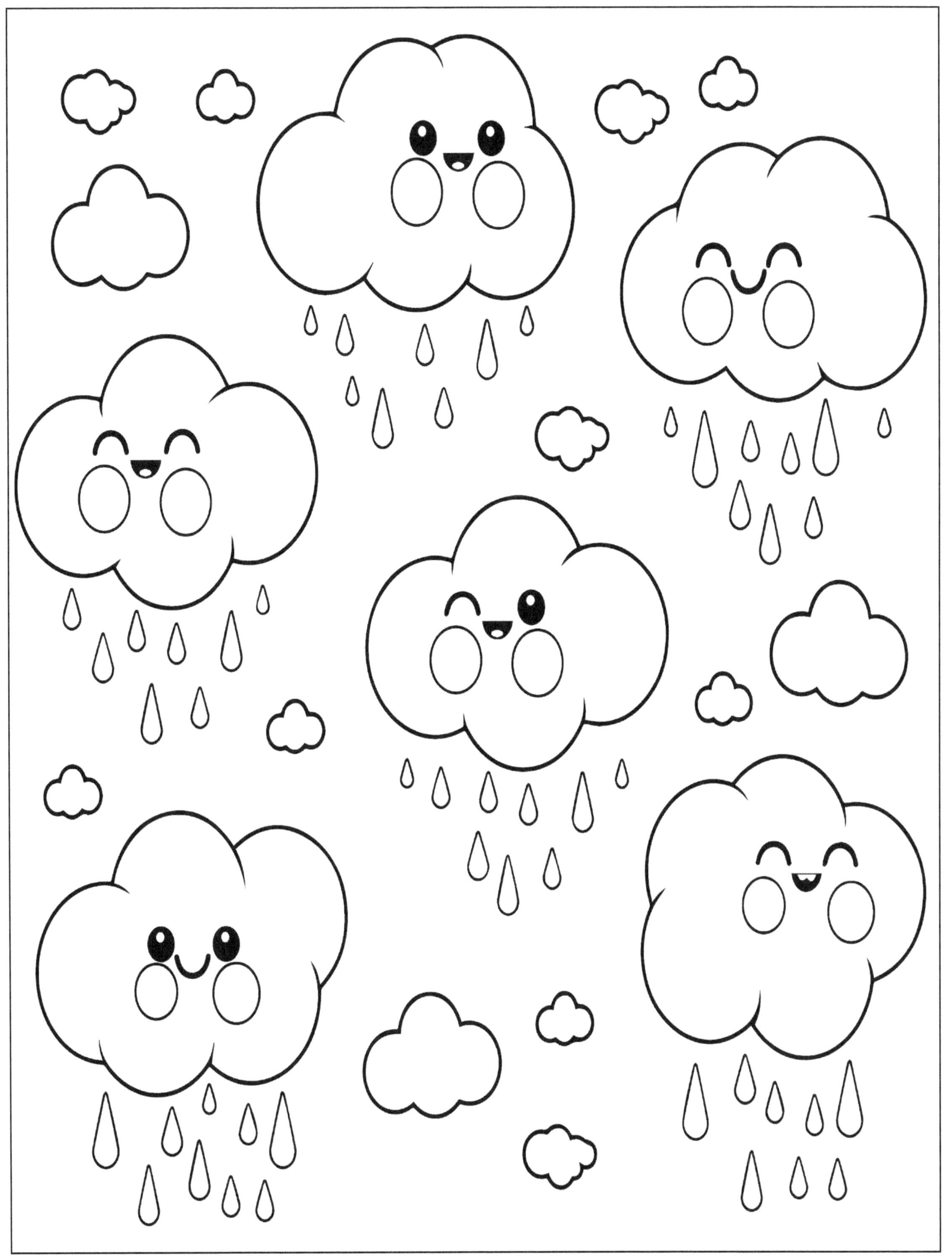

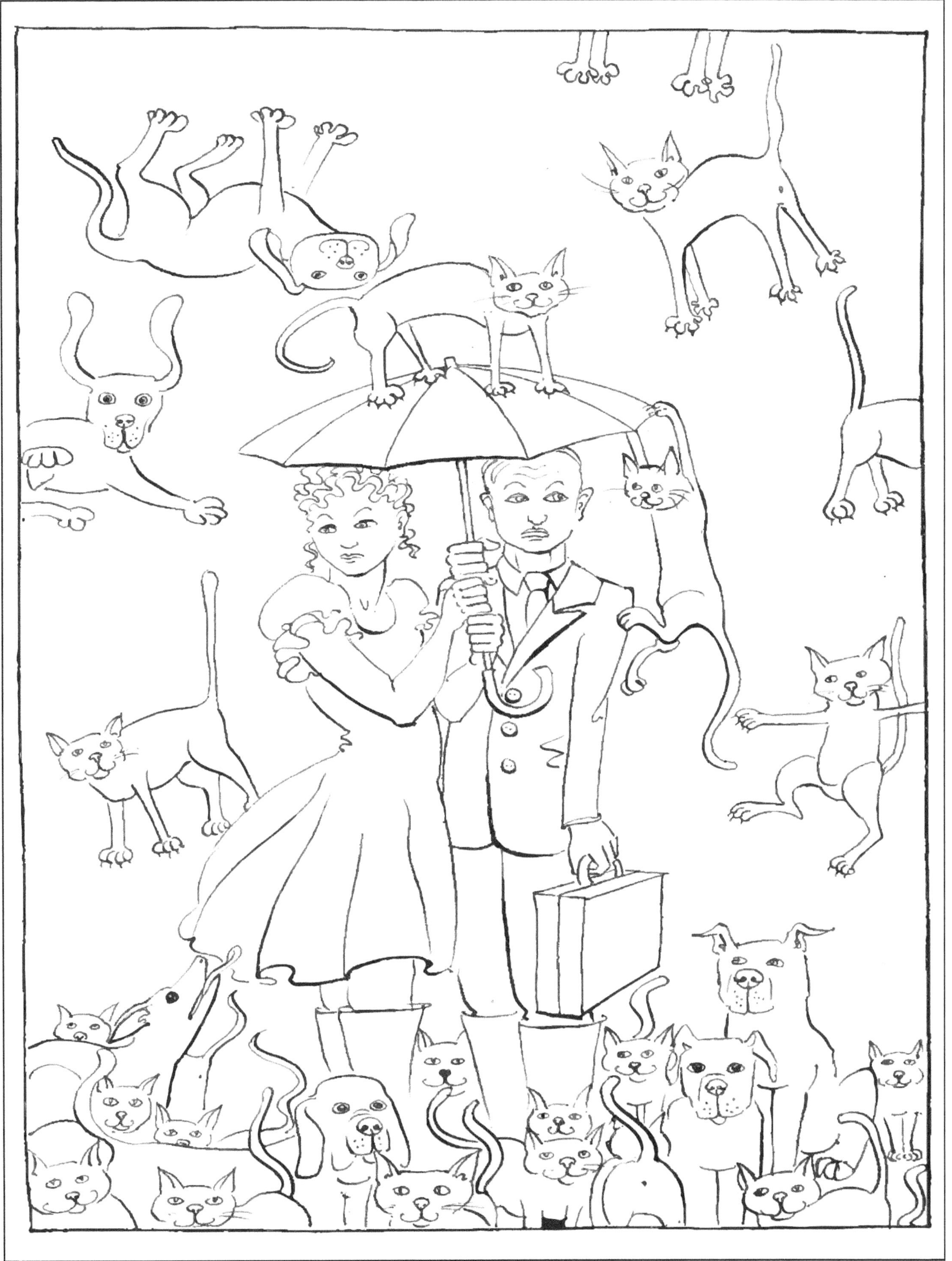

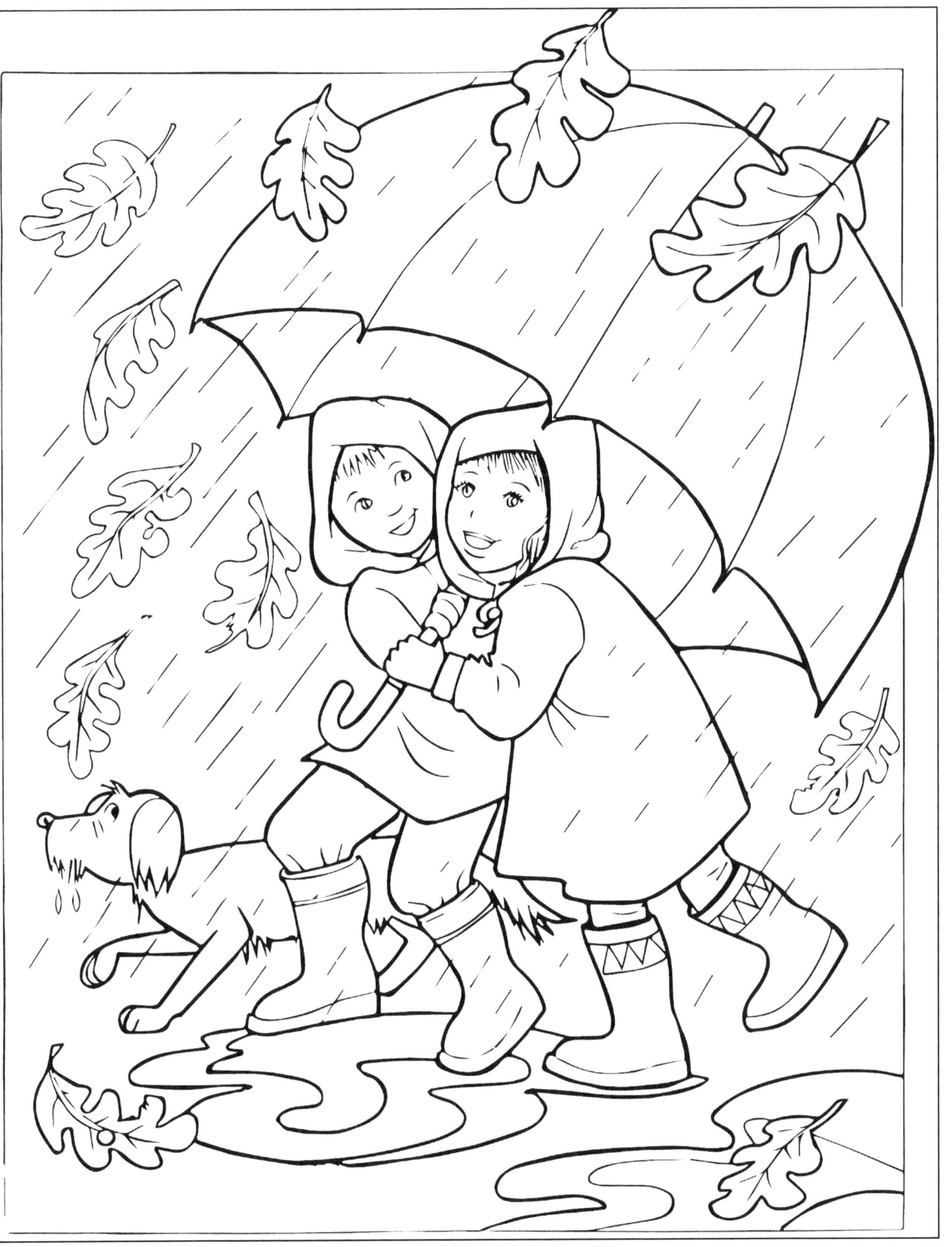

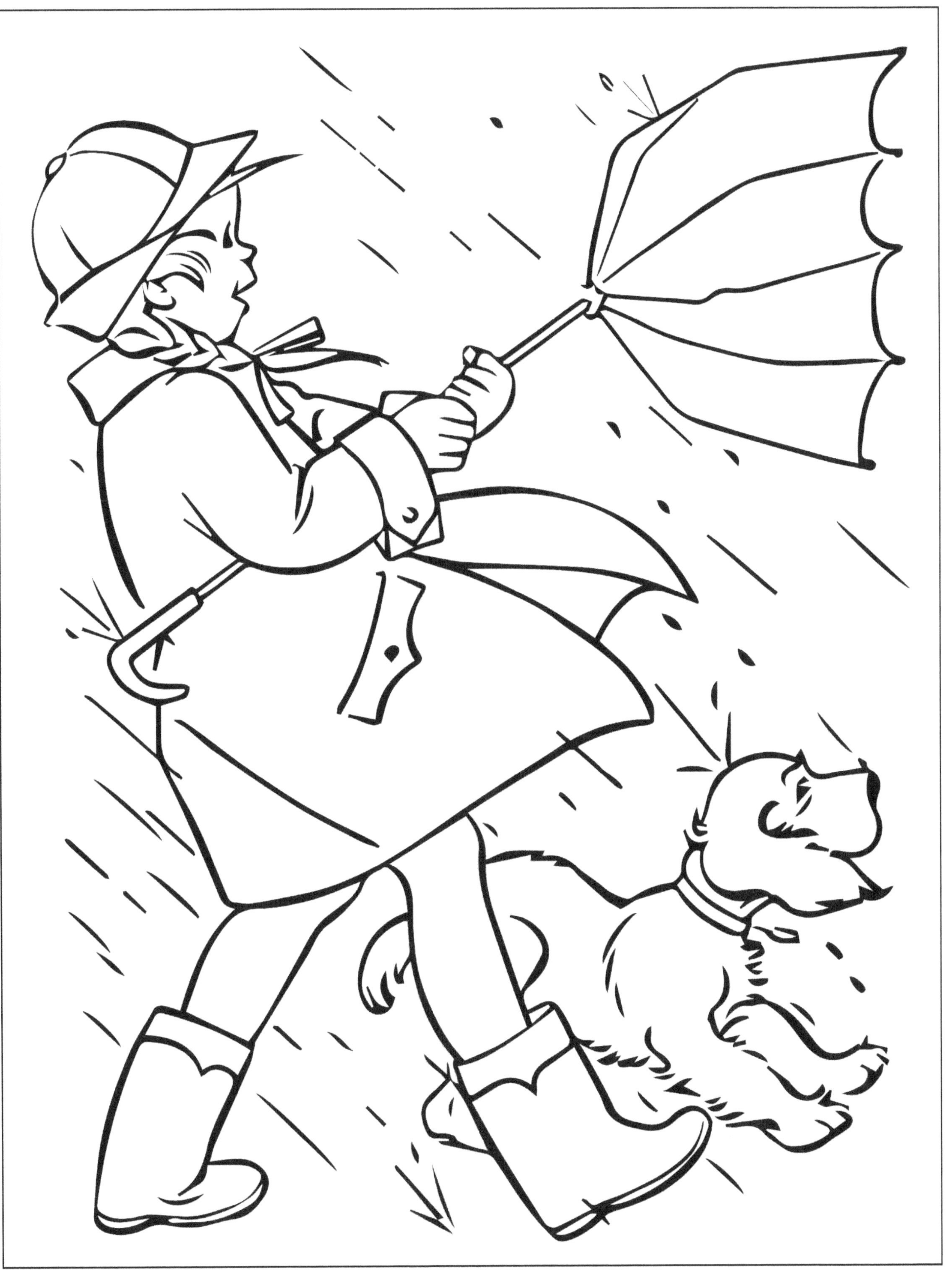

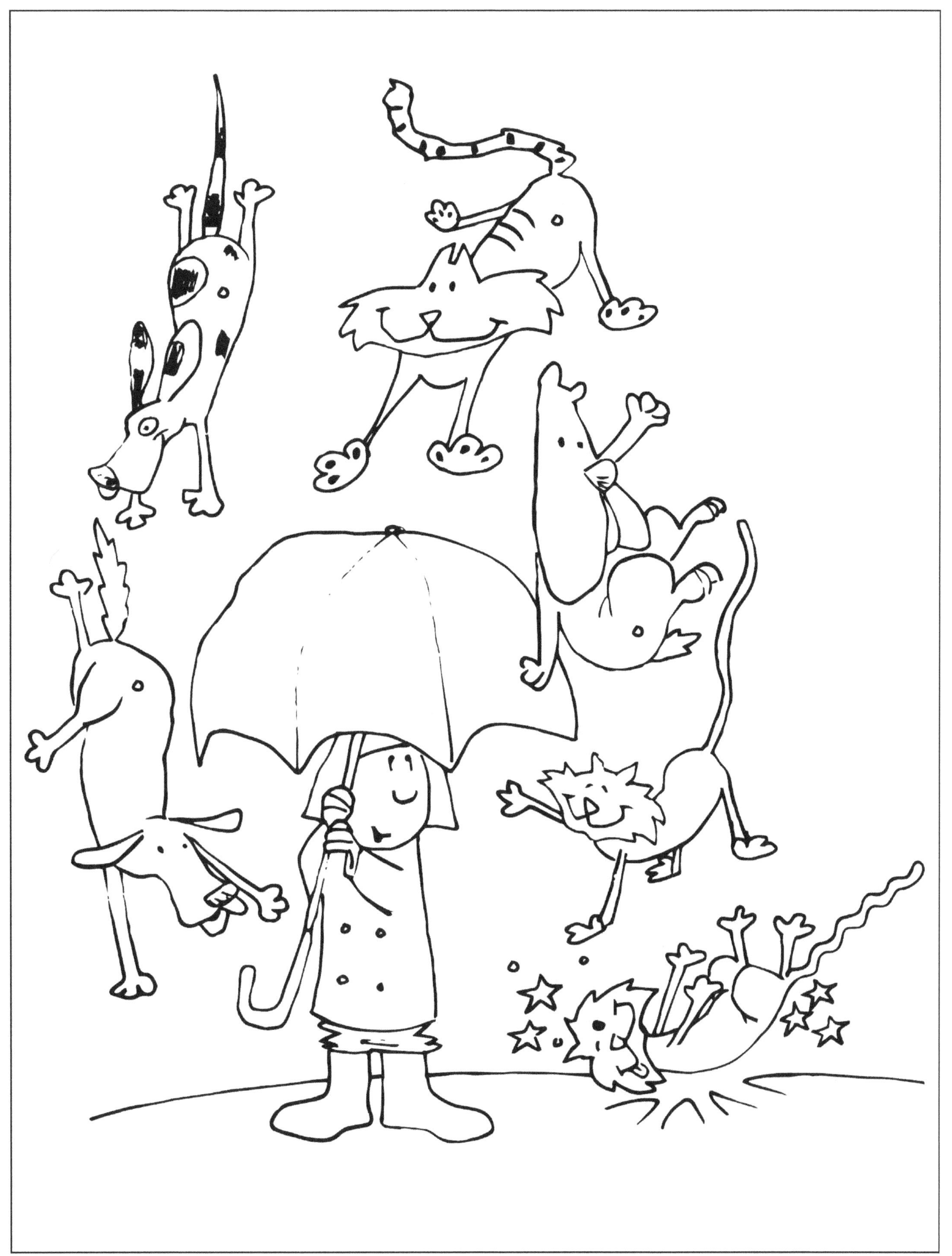

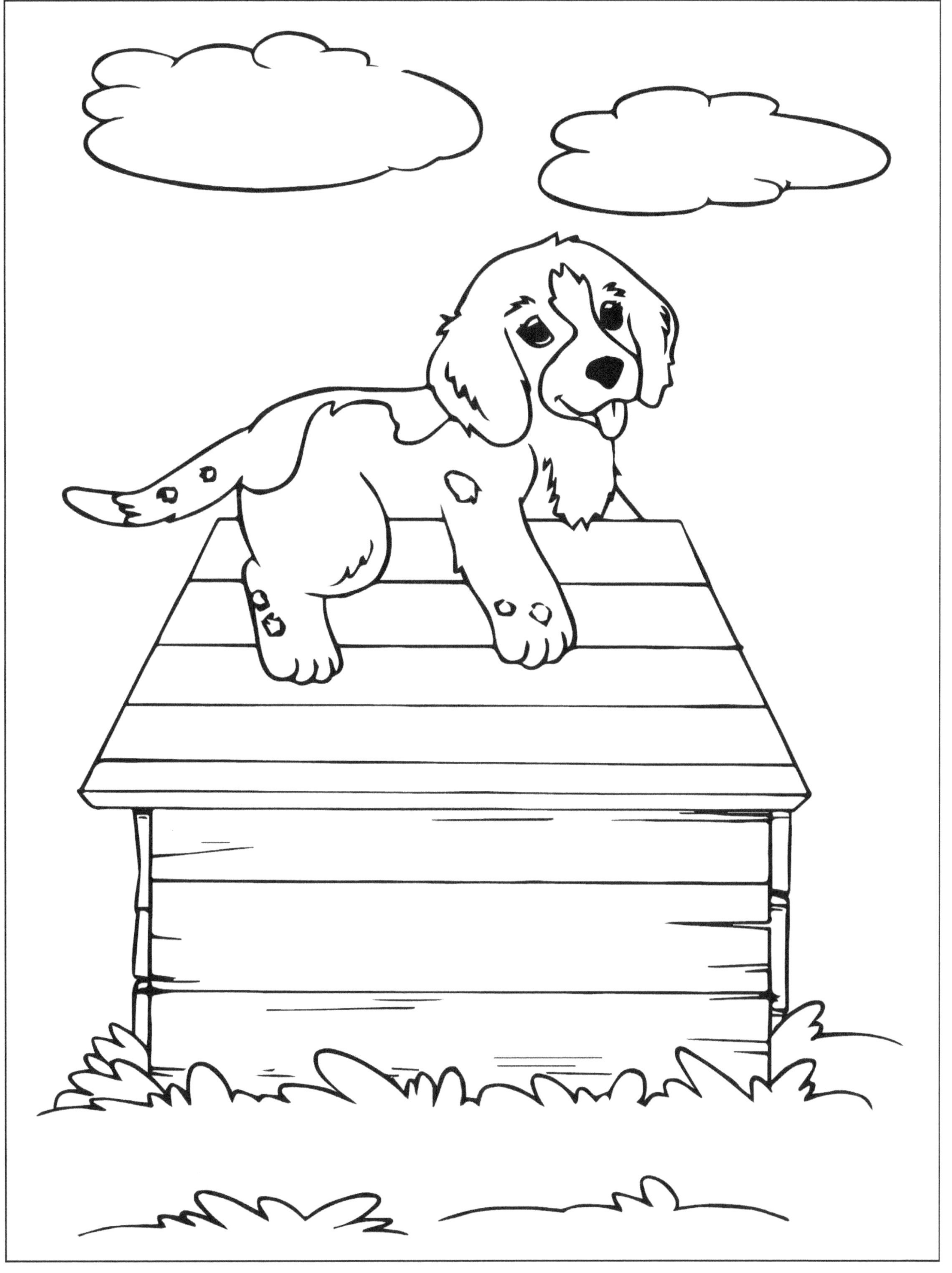

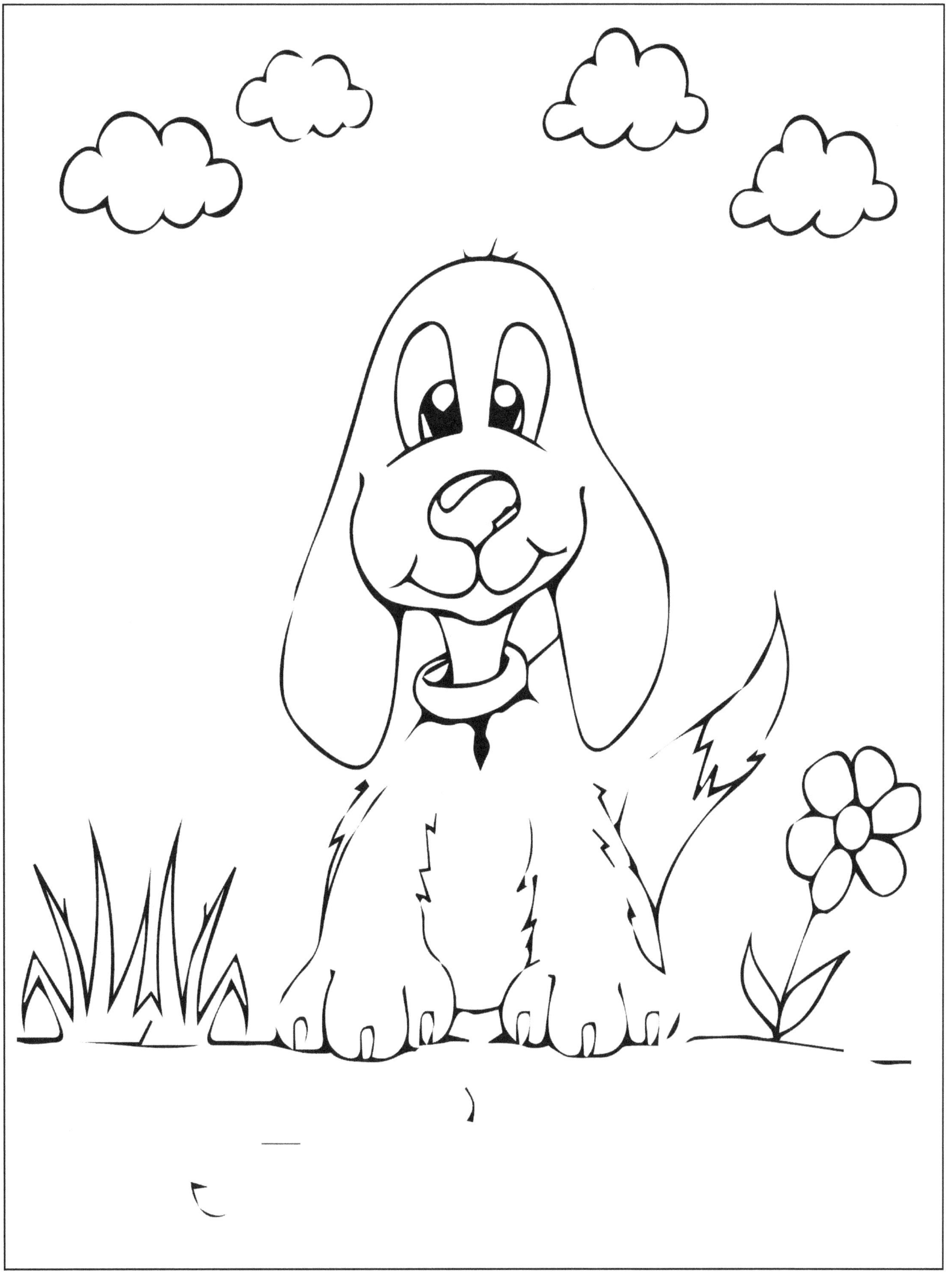

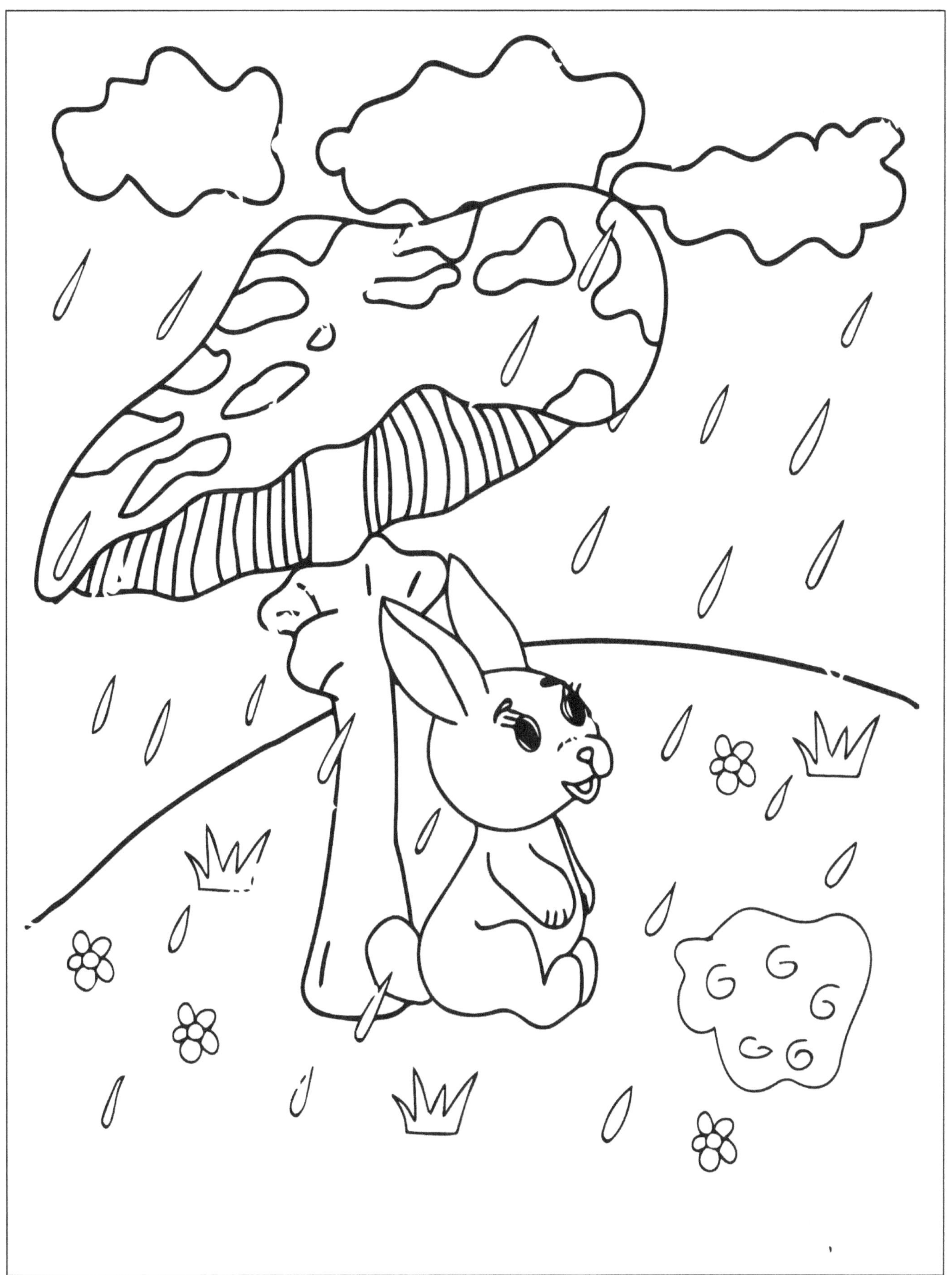

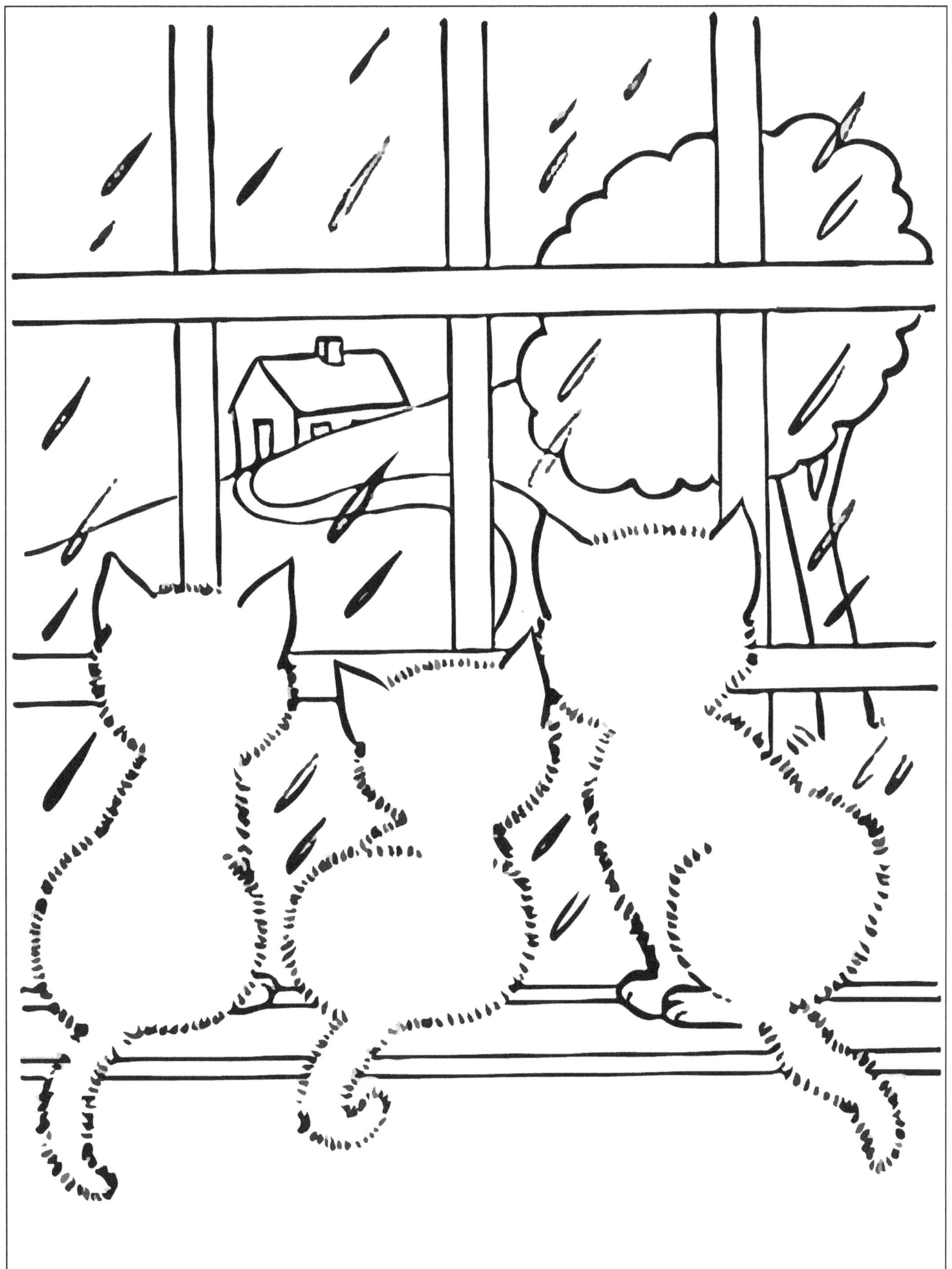

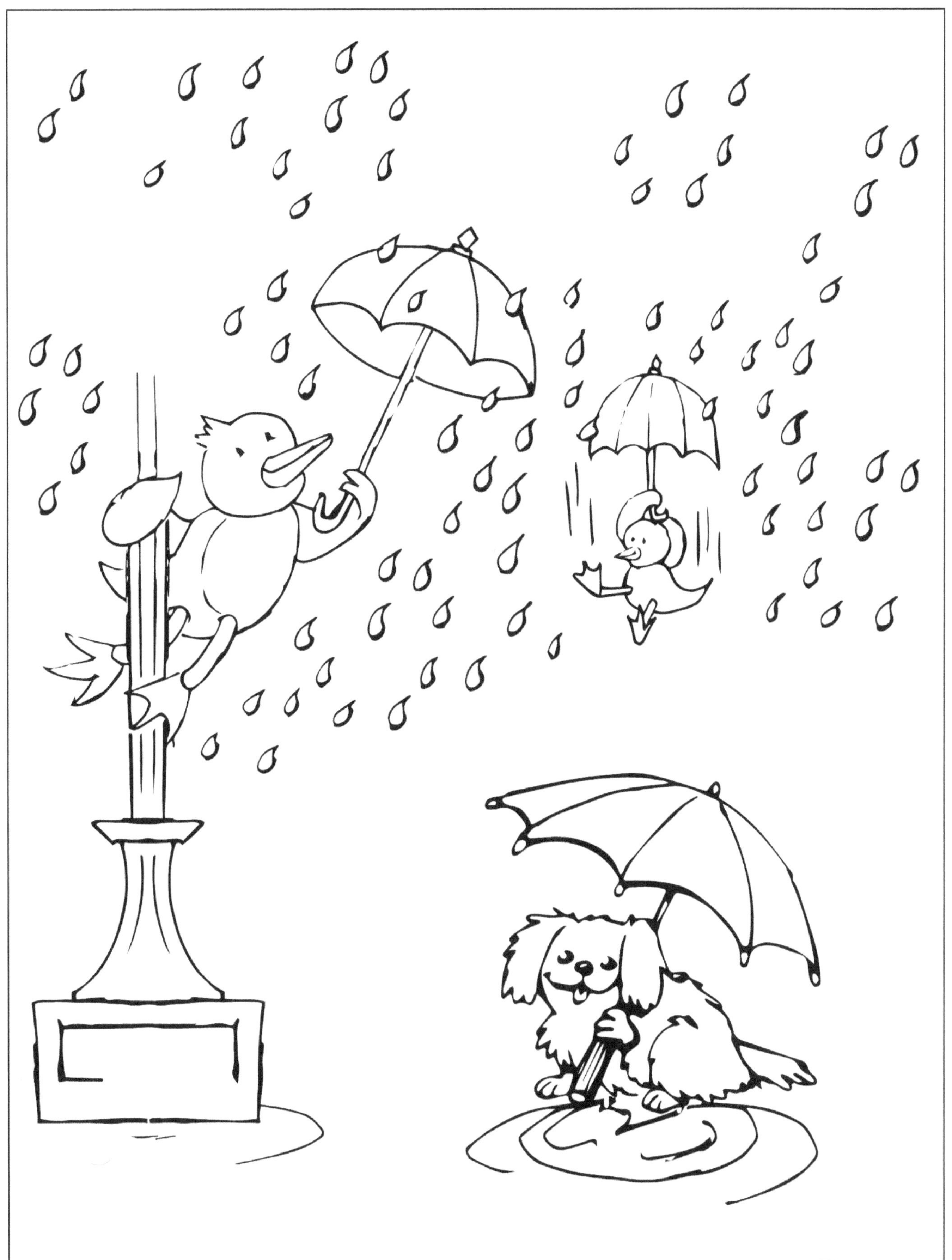

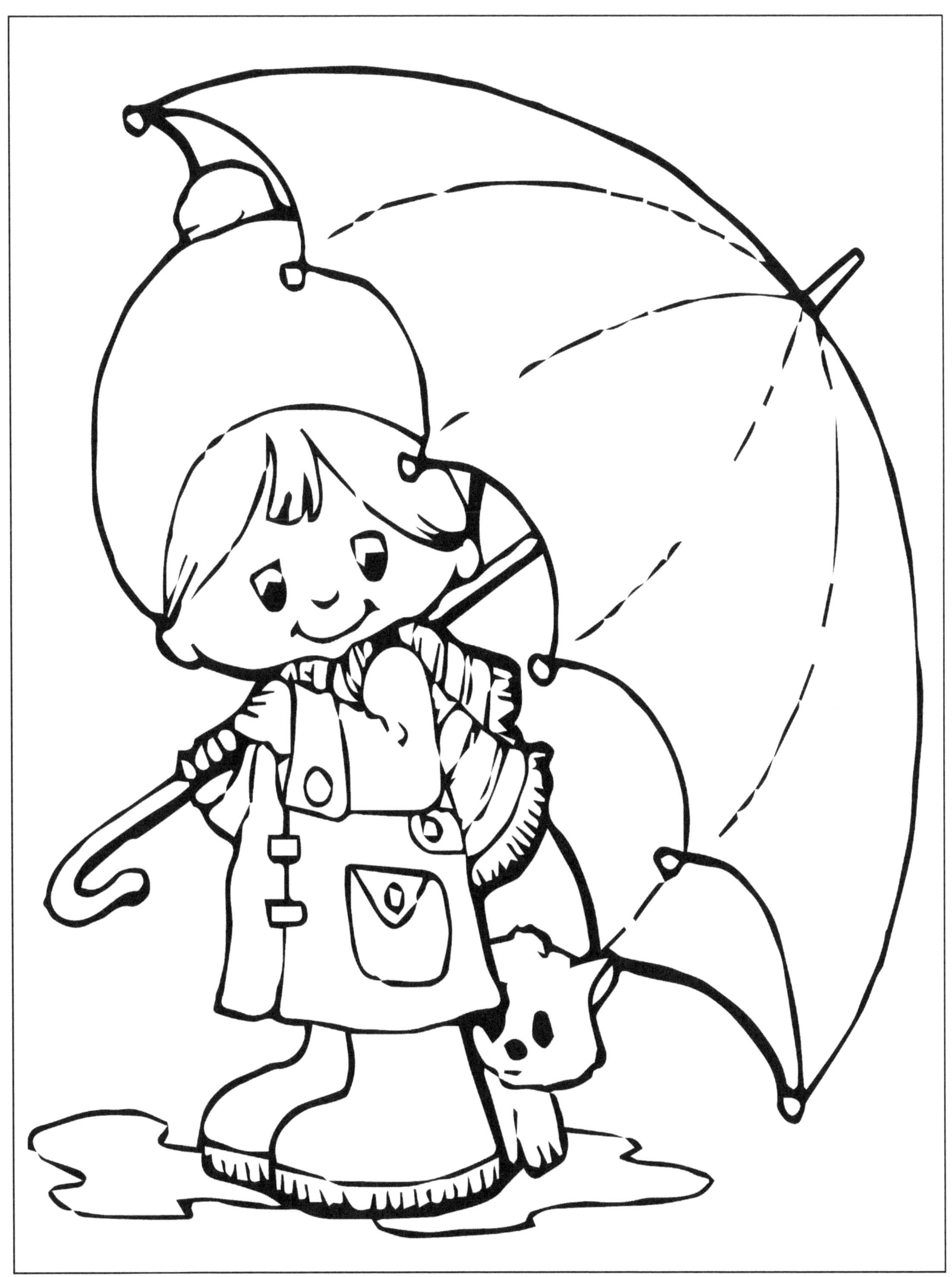

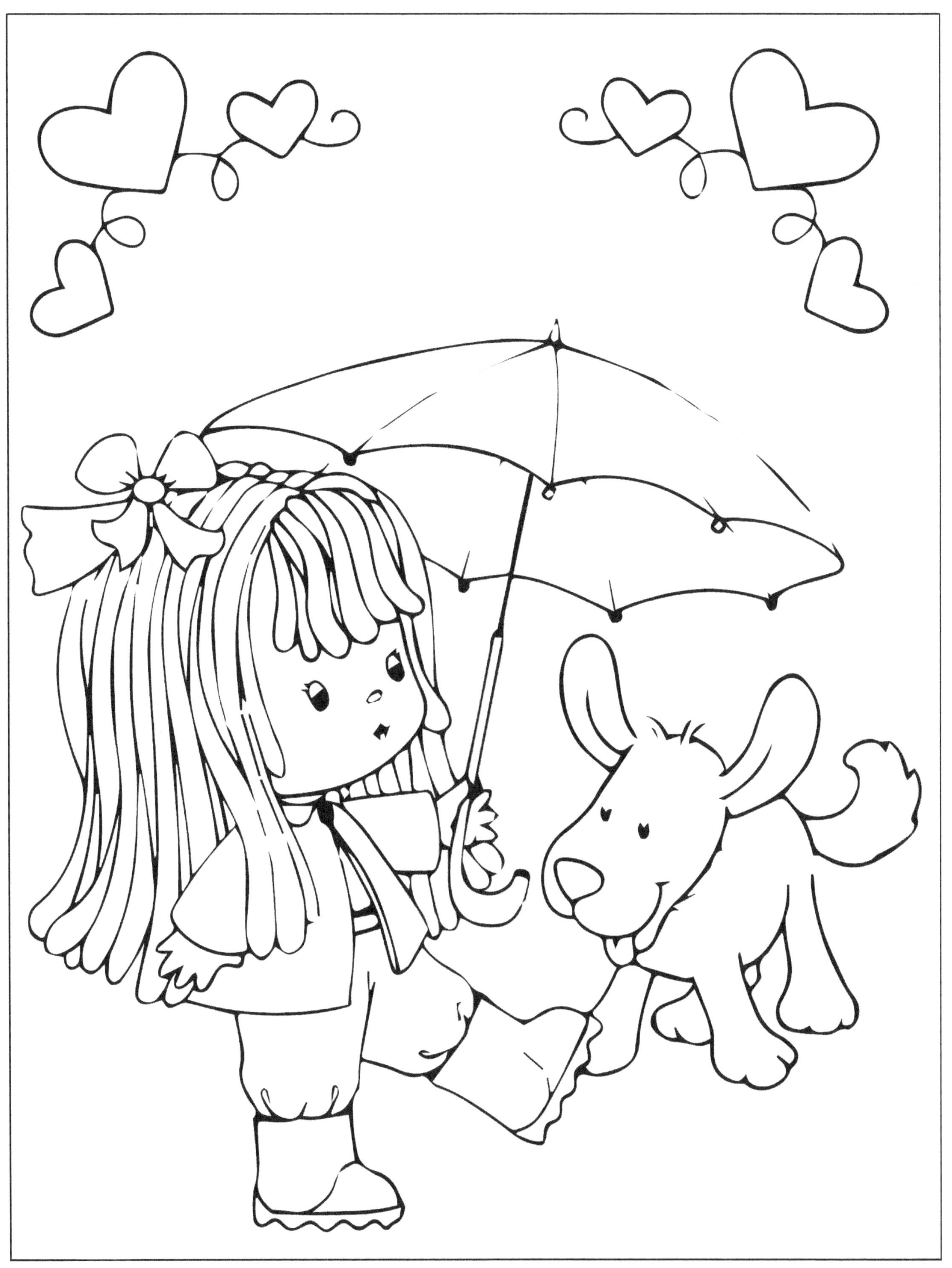

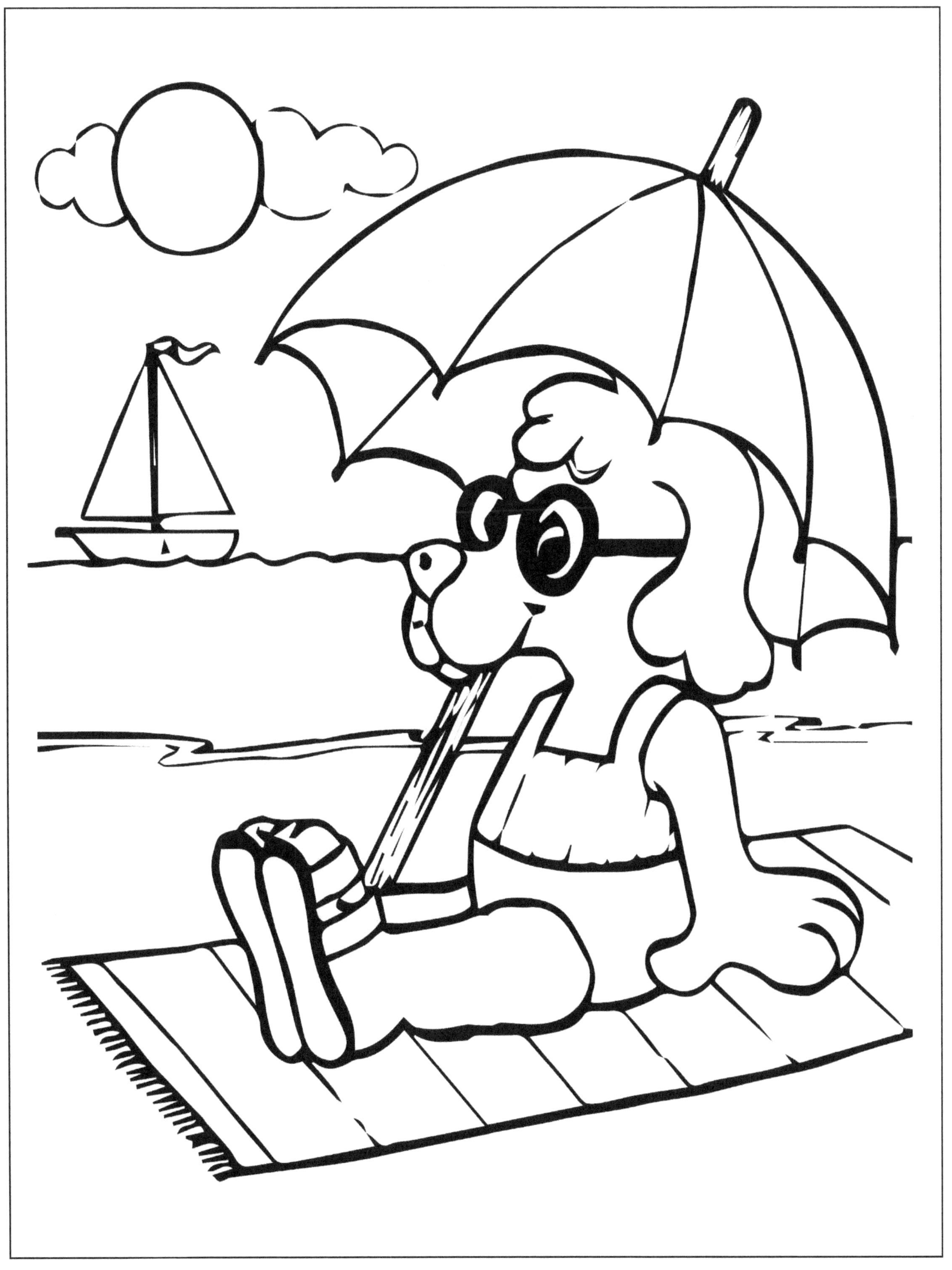

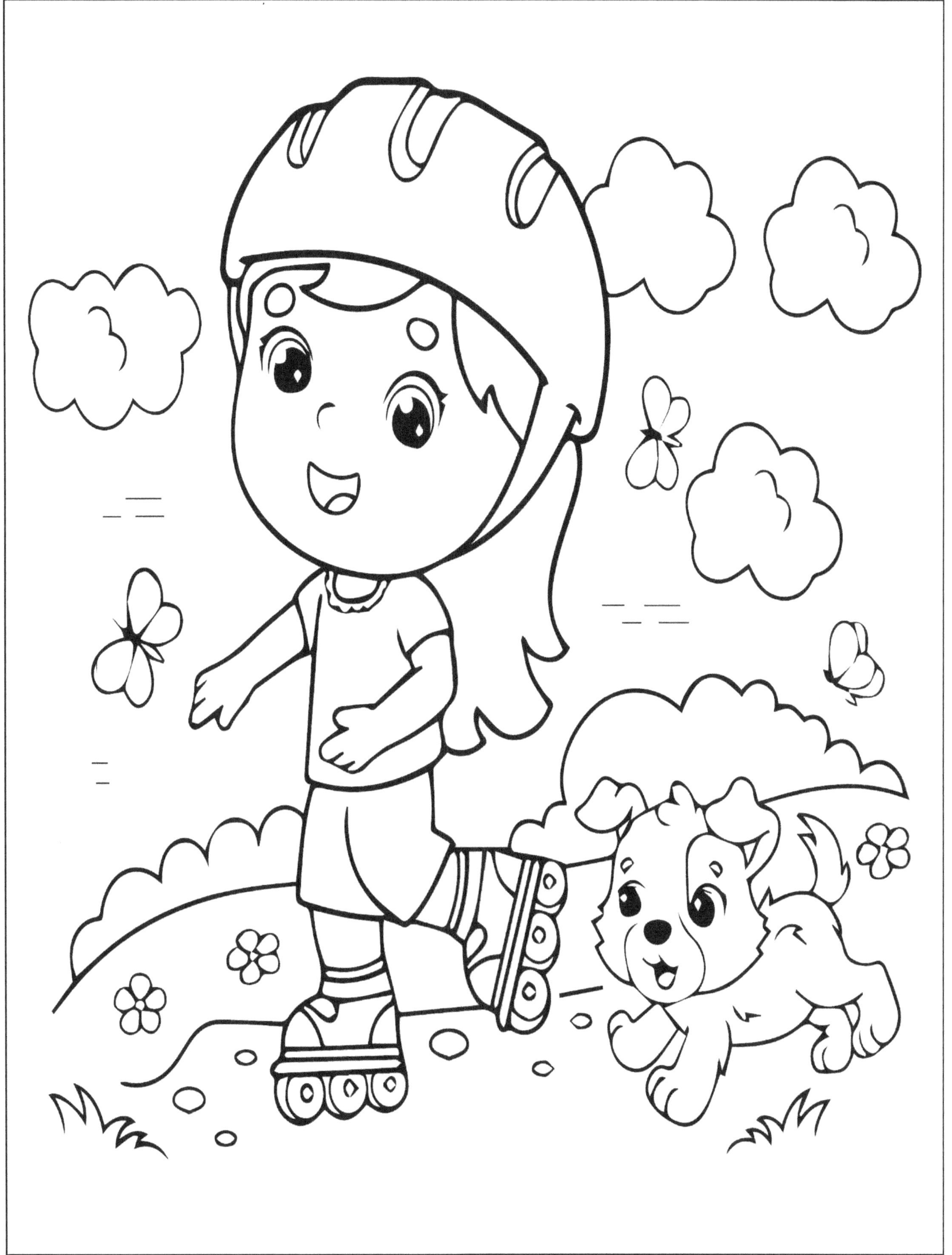

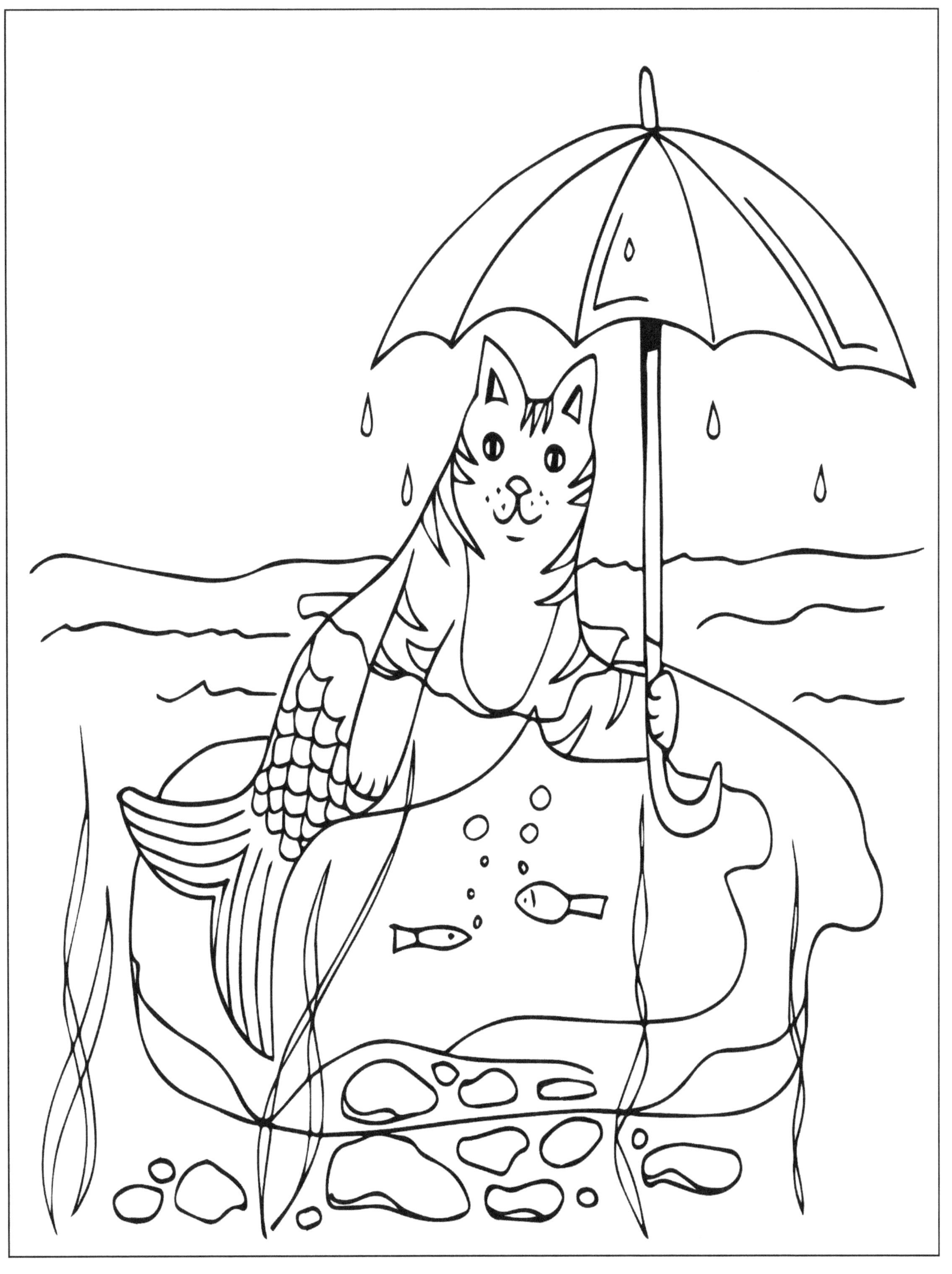

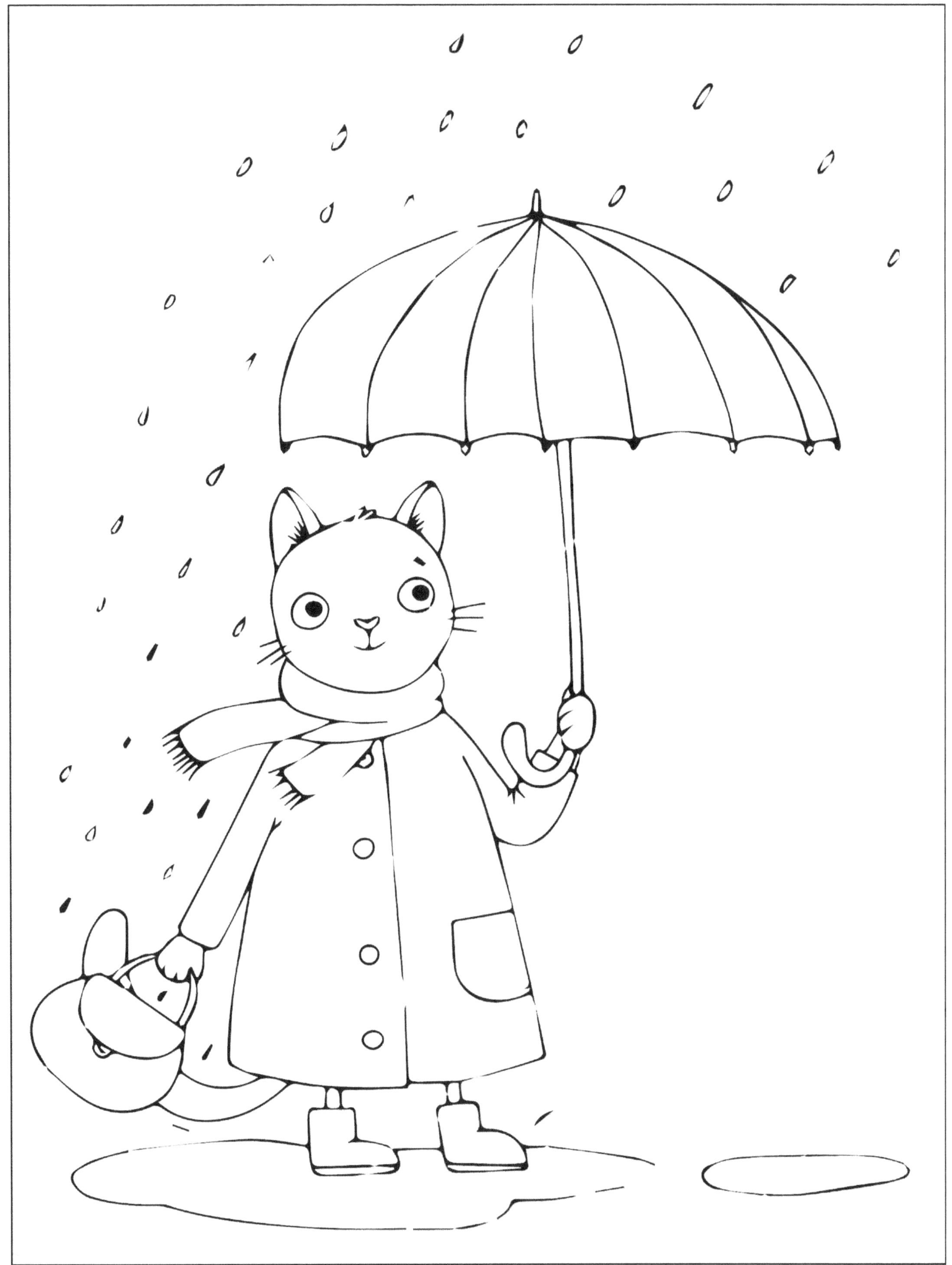

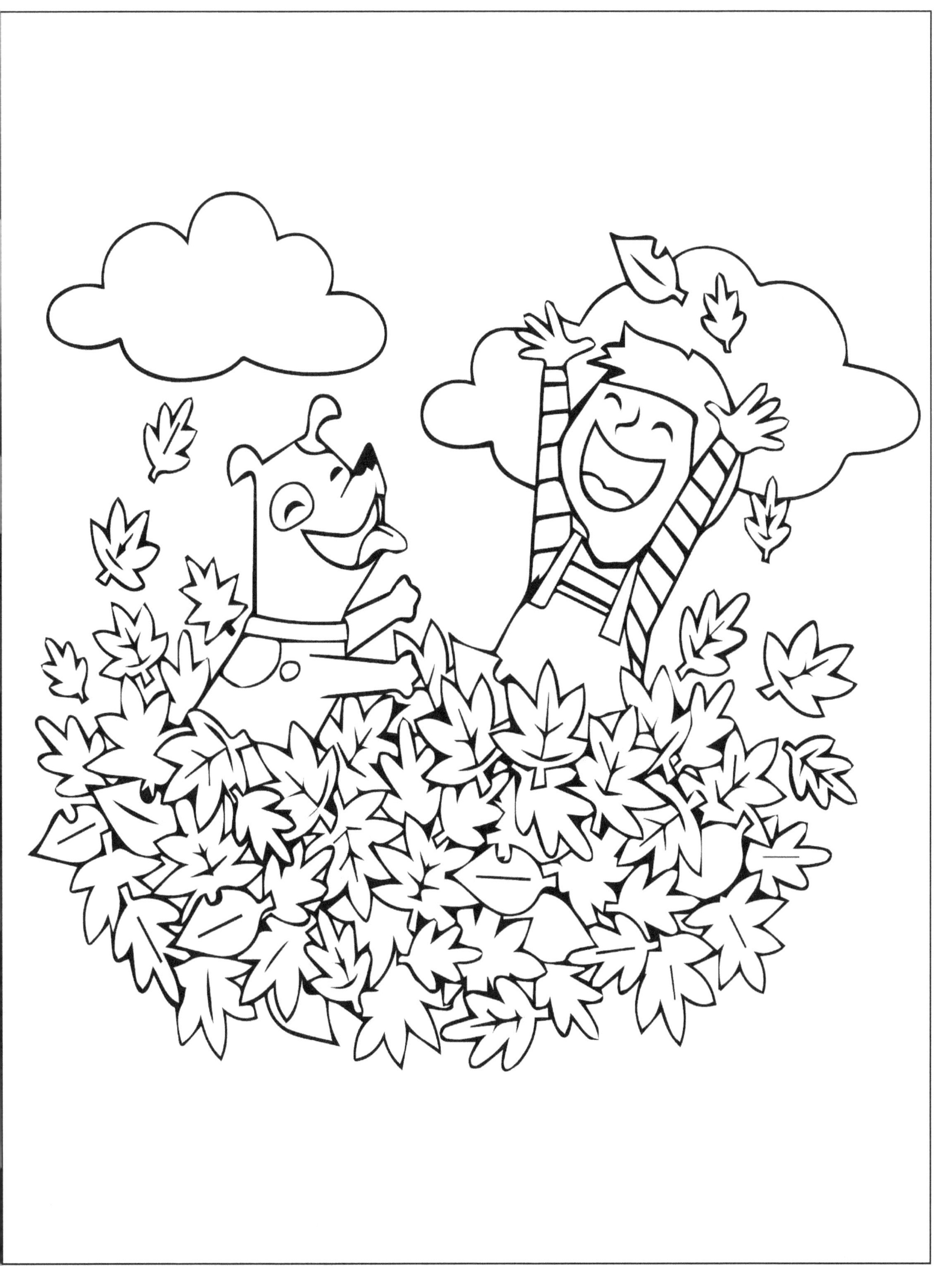

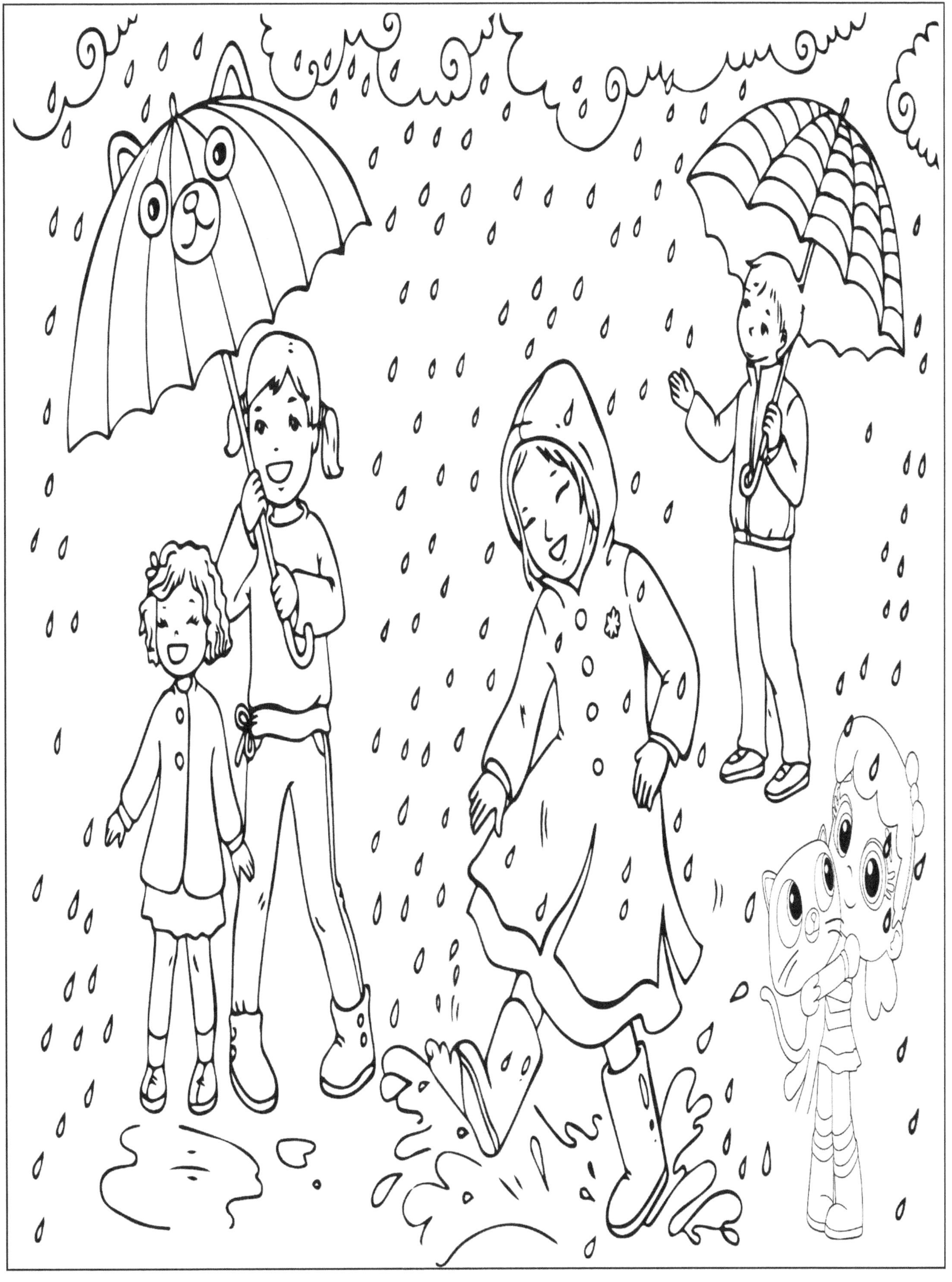

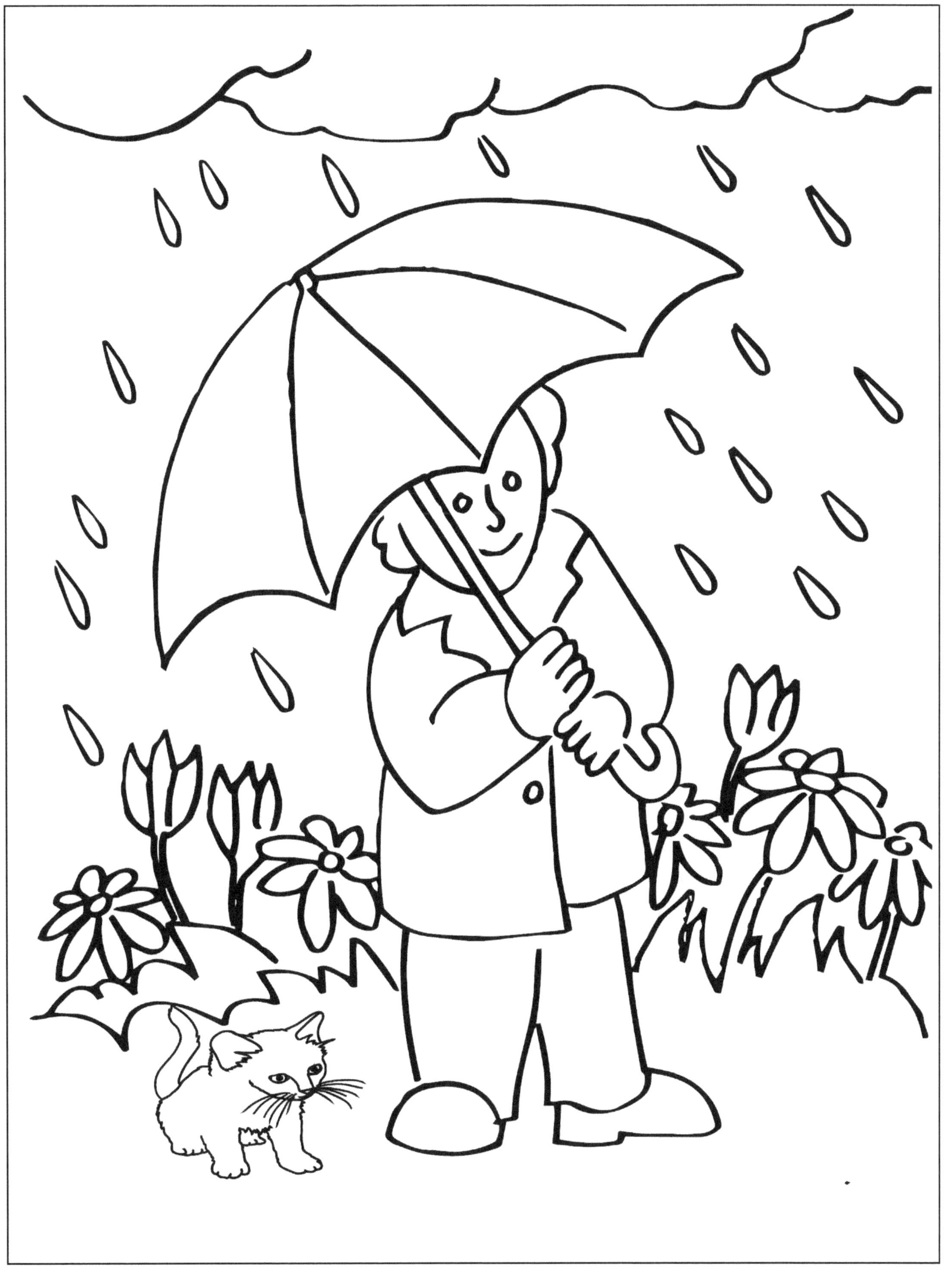

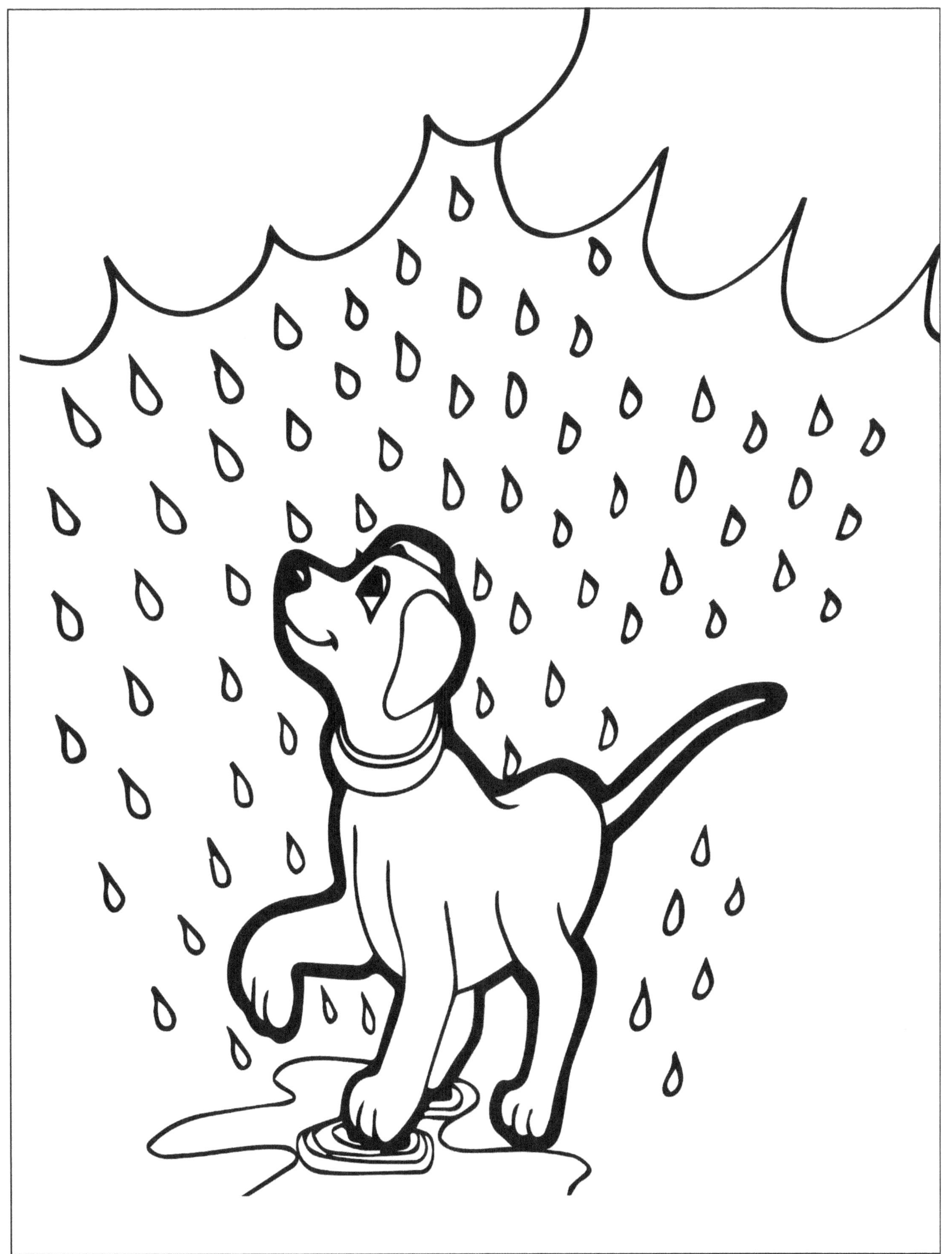

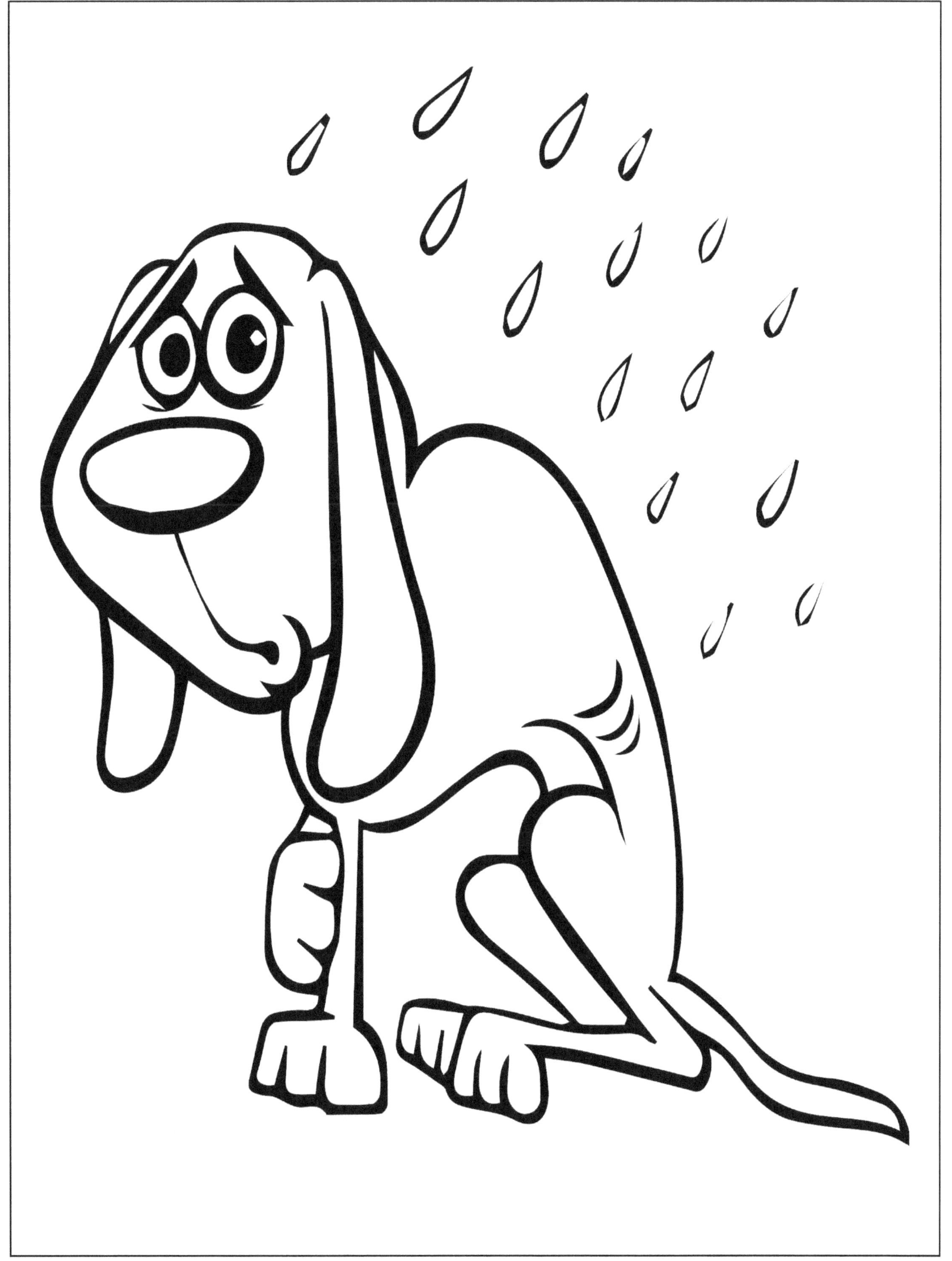

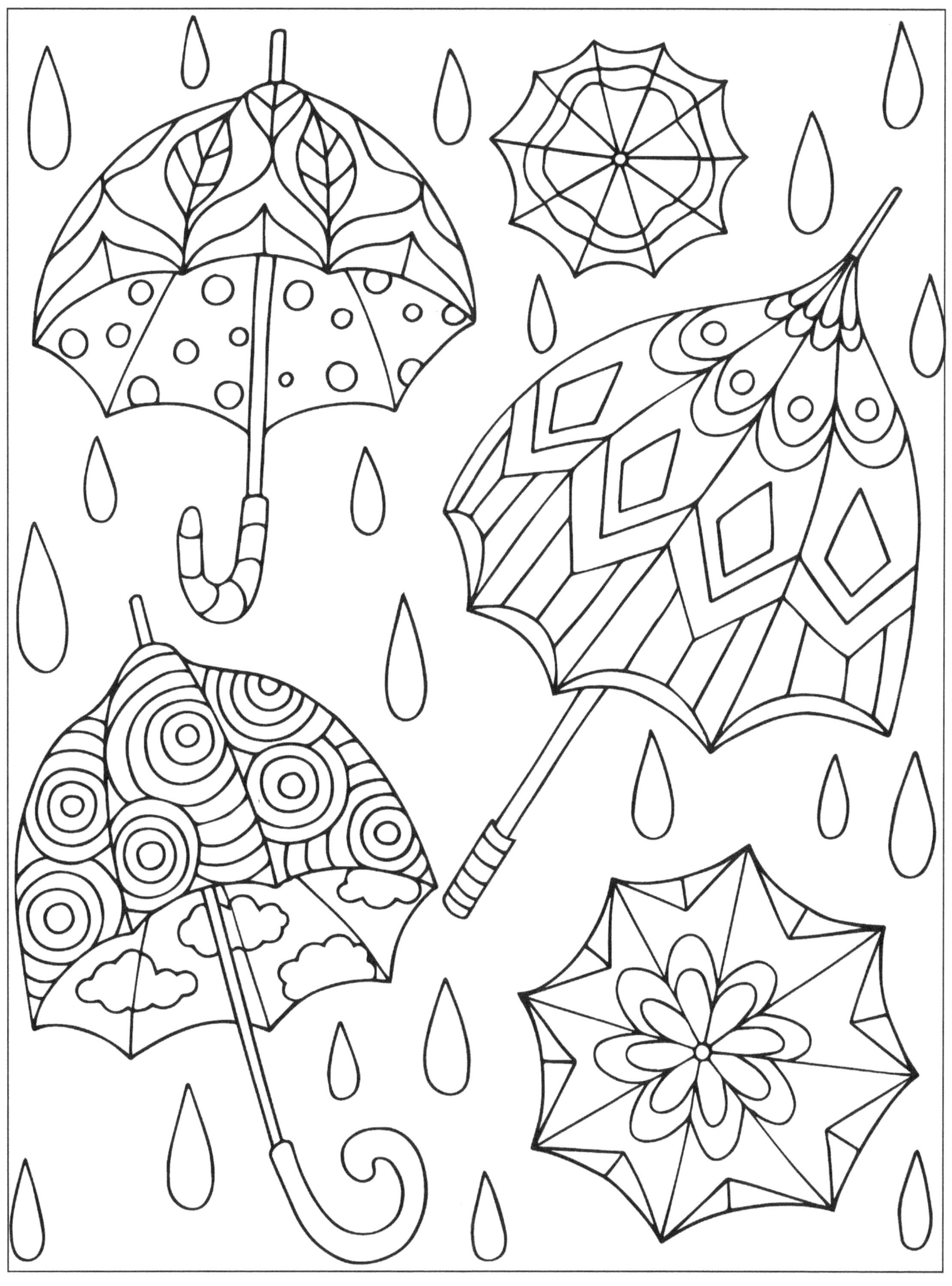

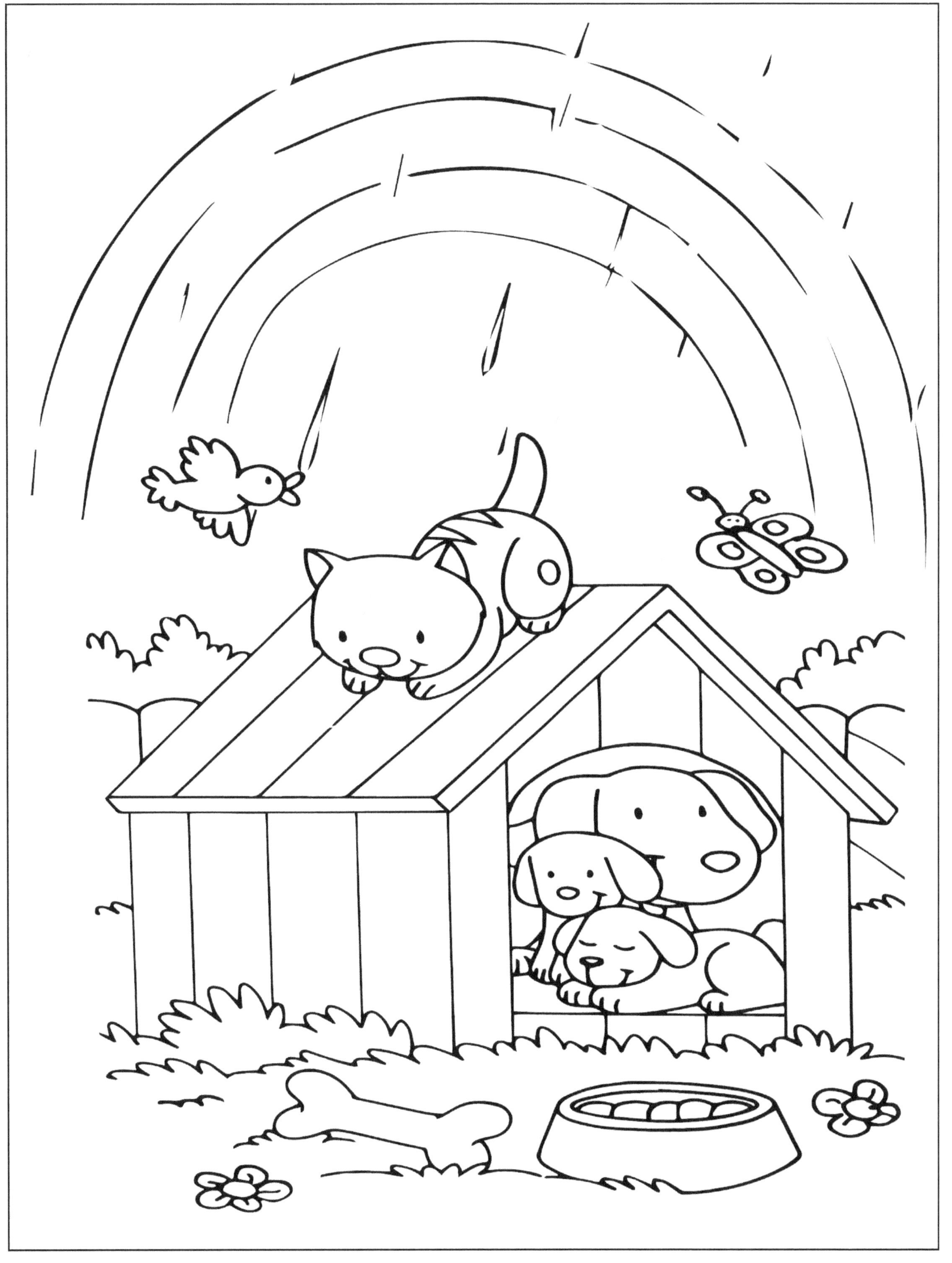

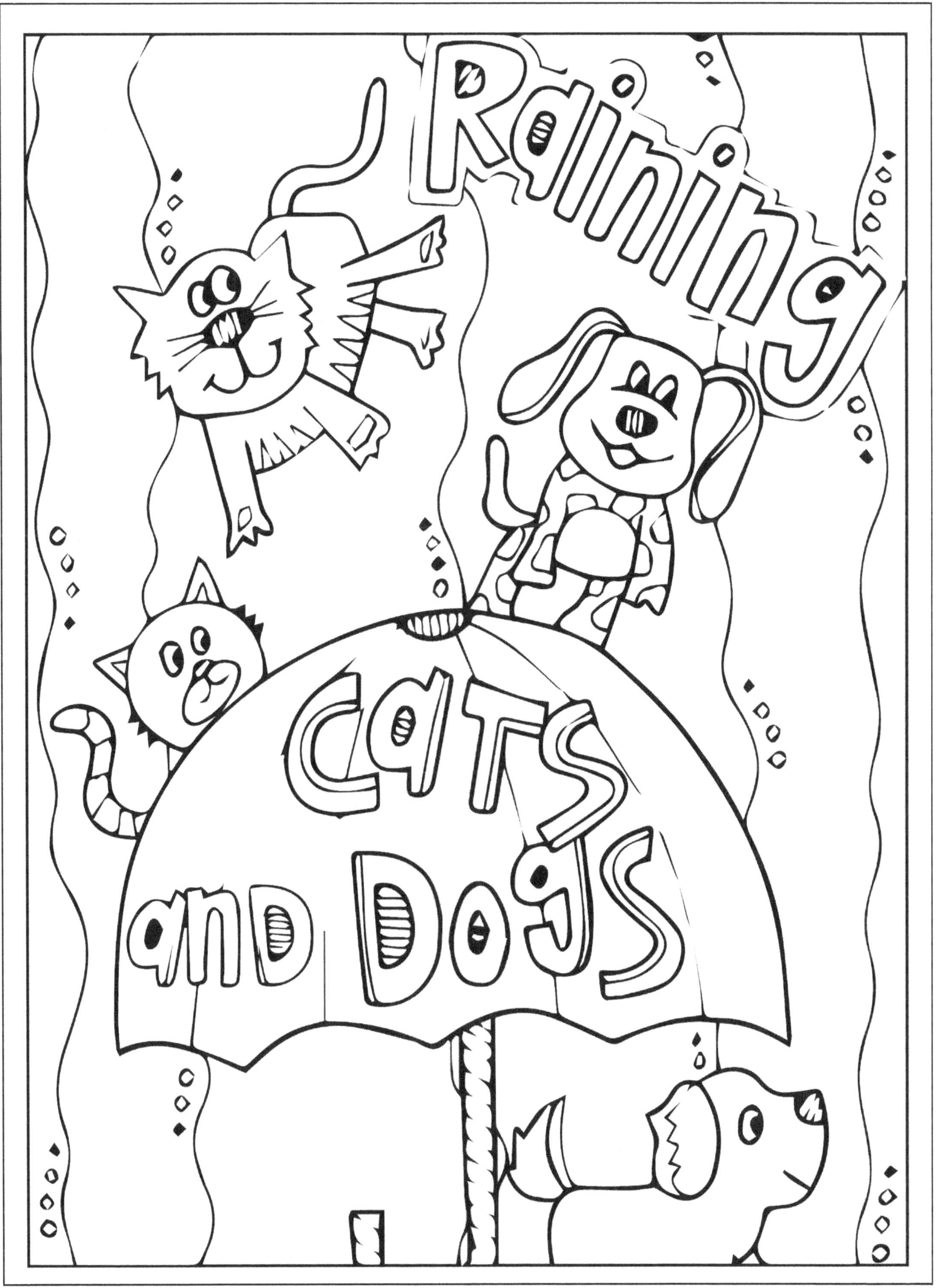

Raining
Cats
and Dogs

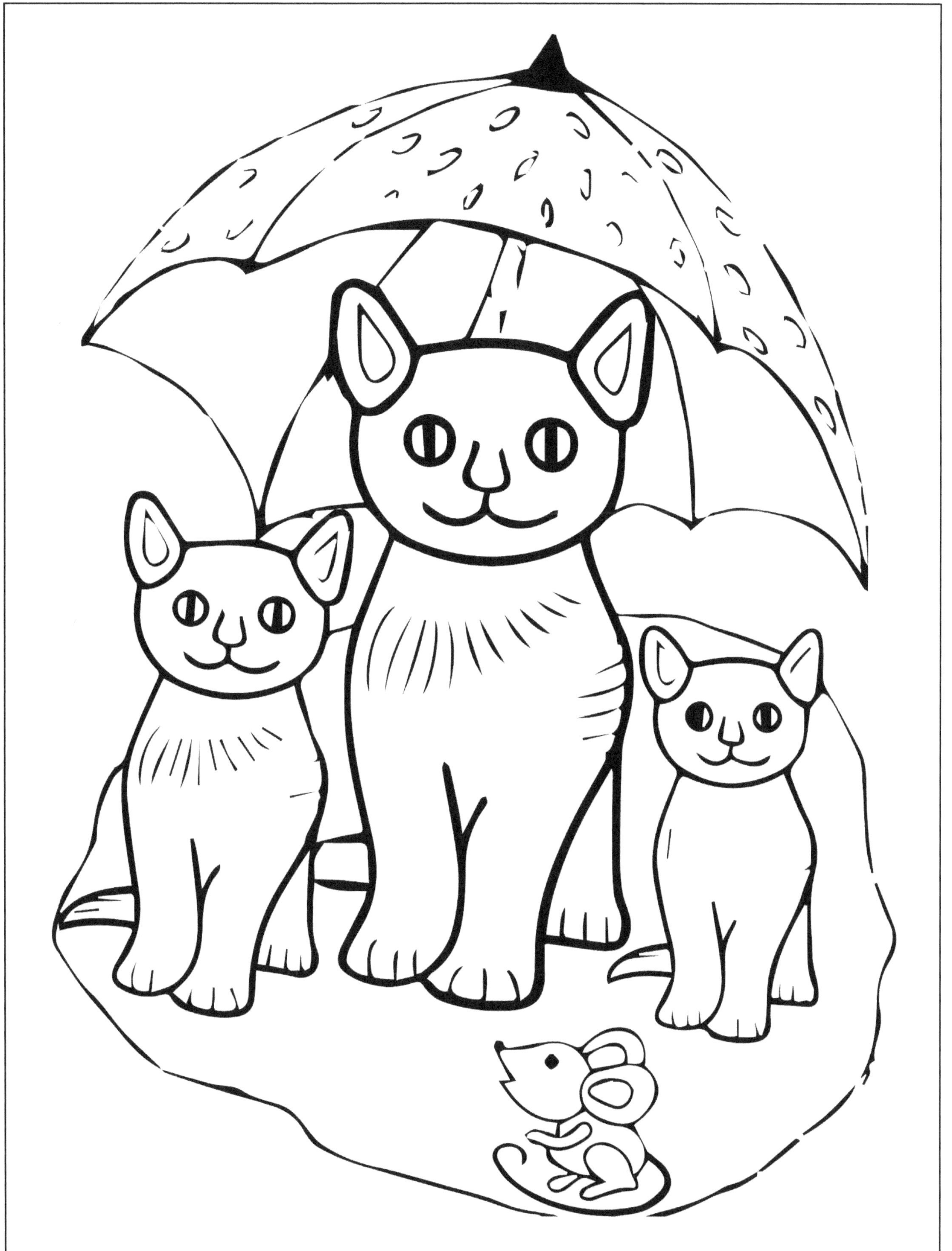

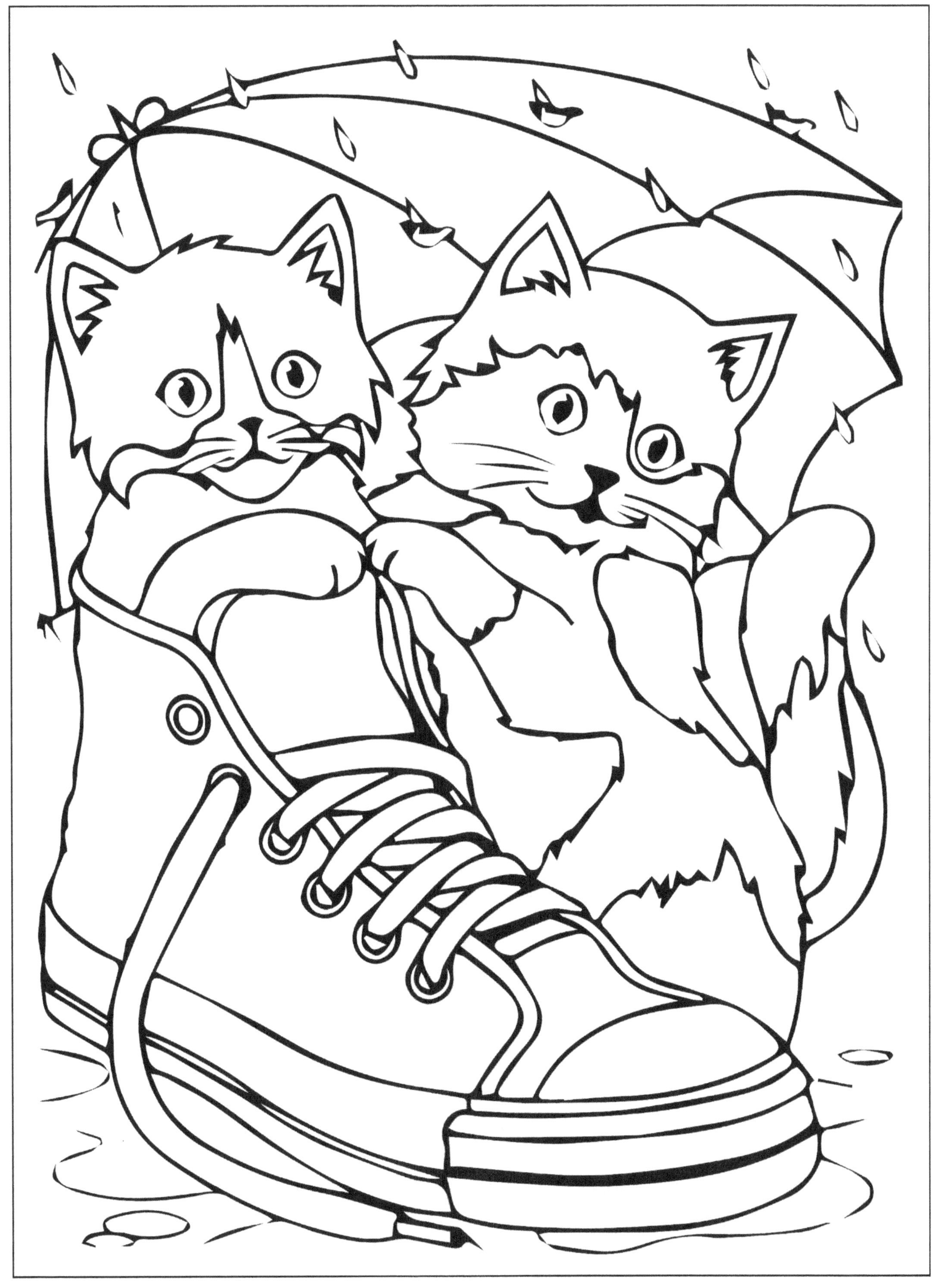

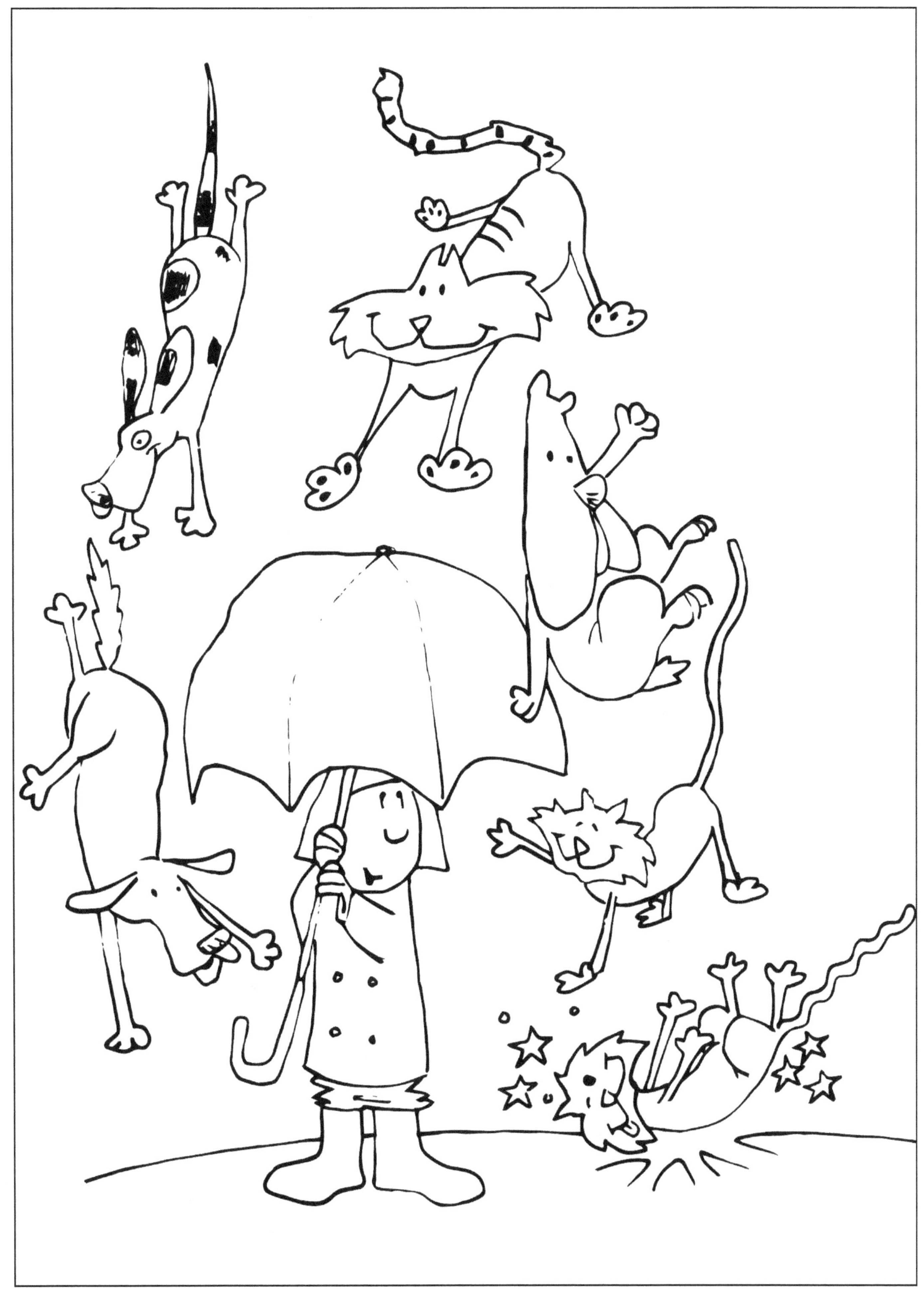

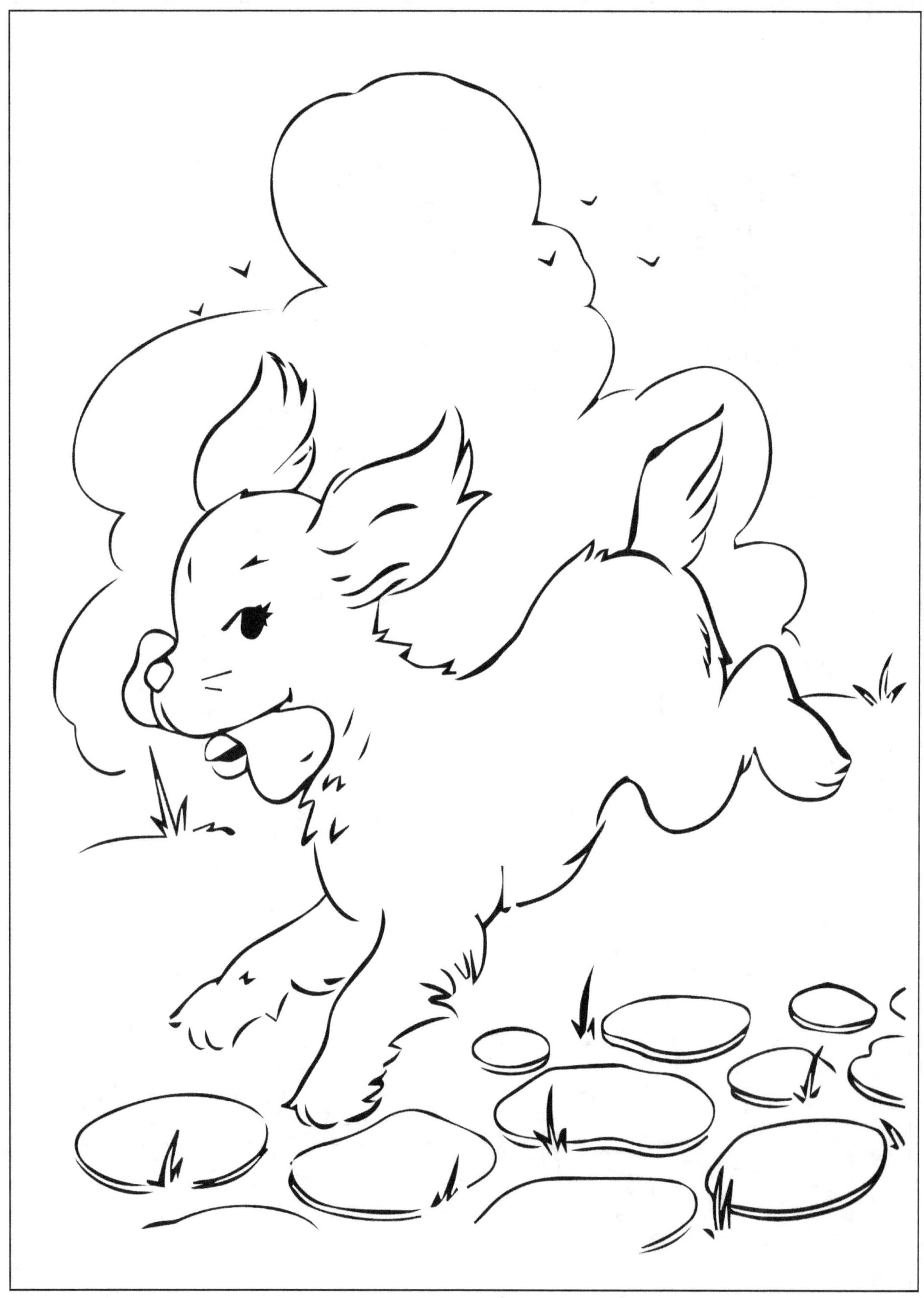

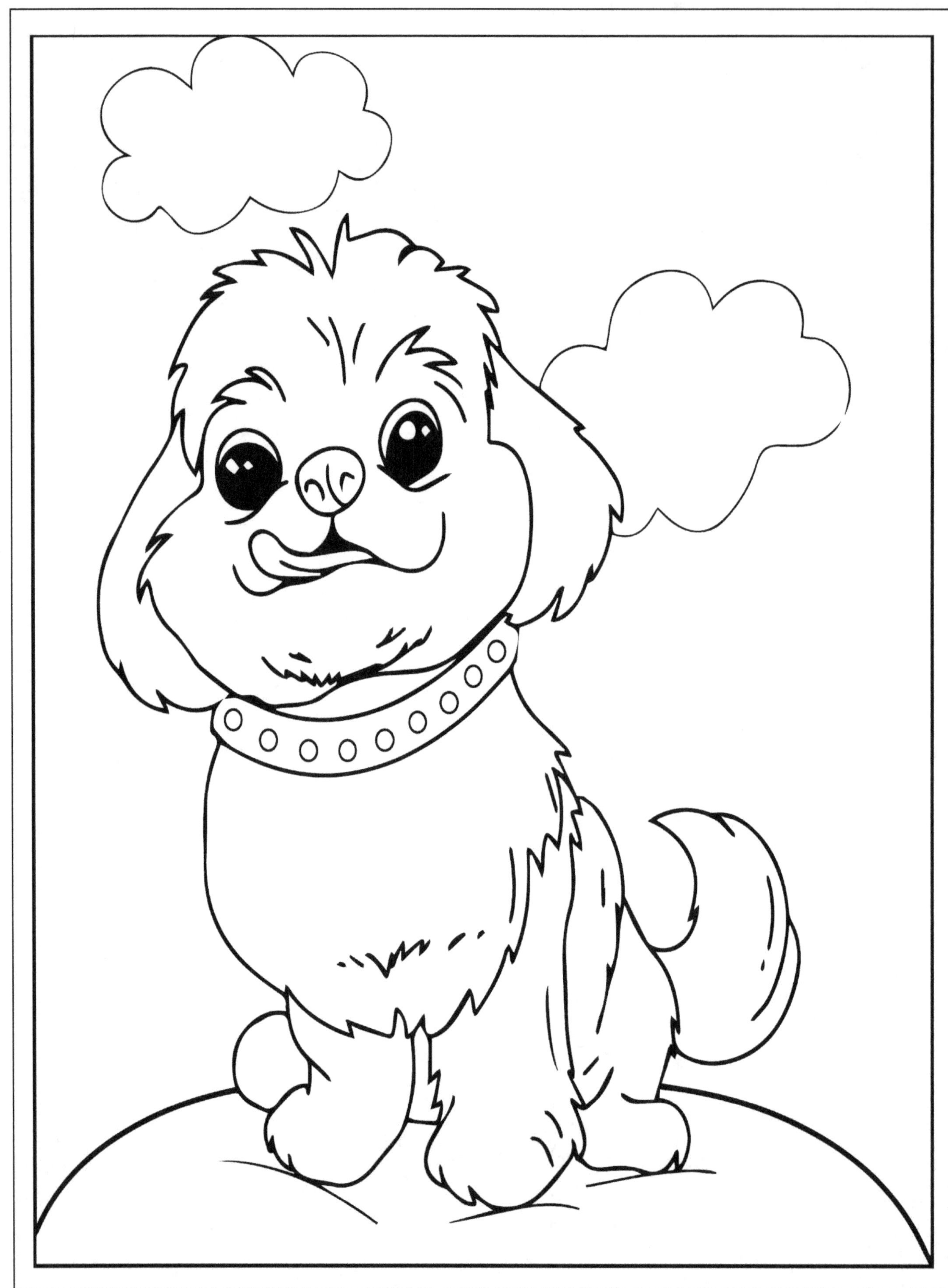

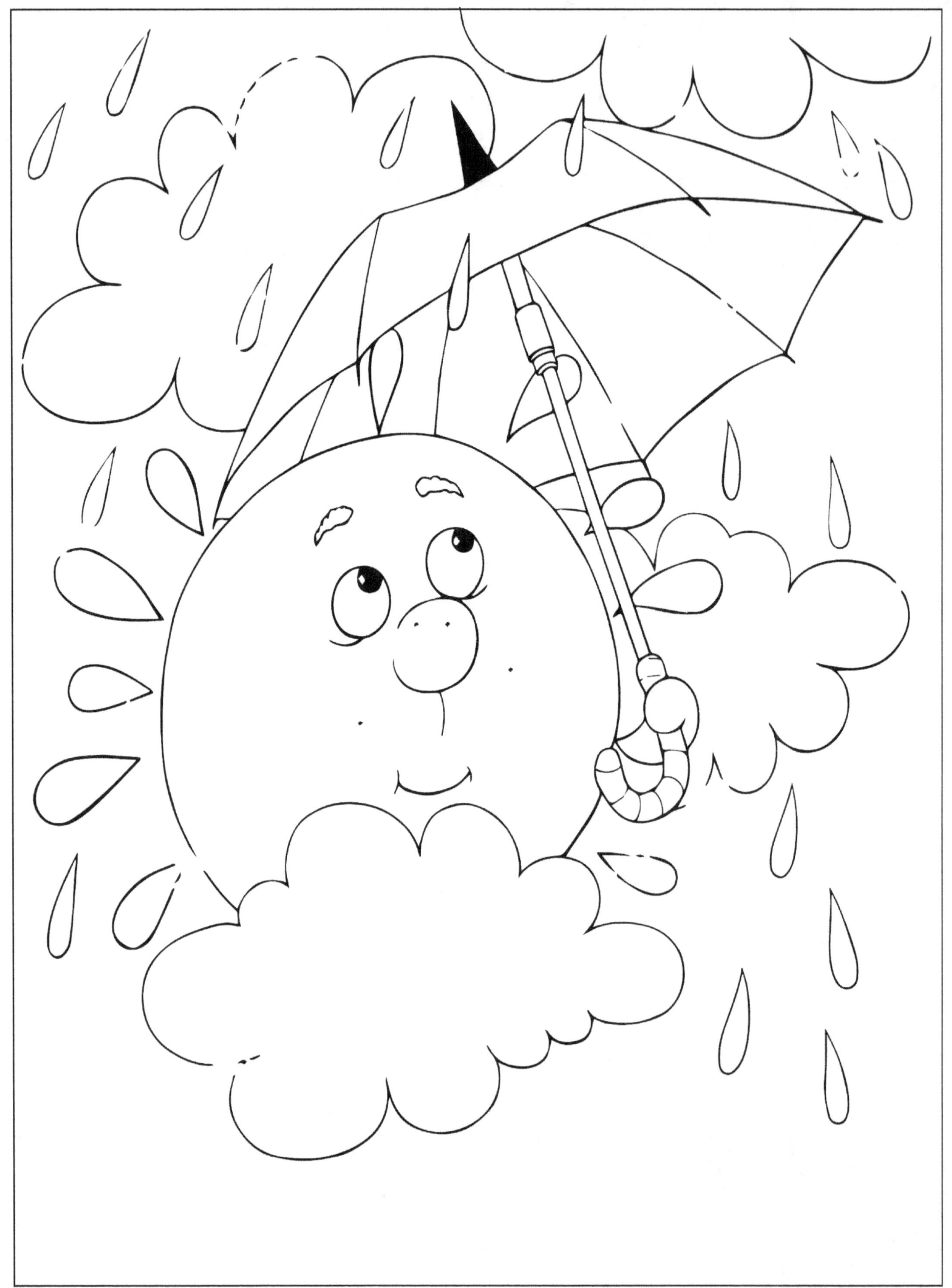

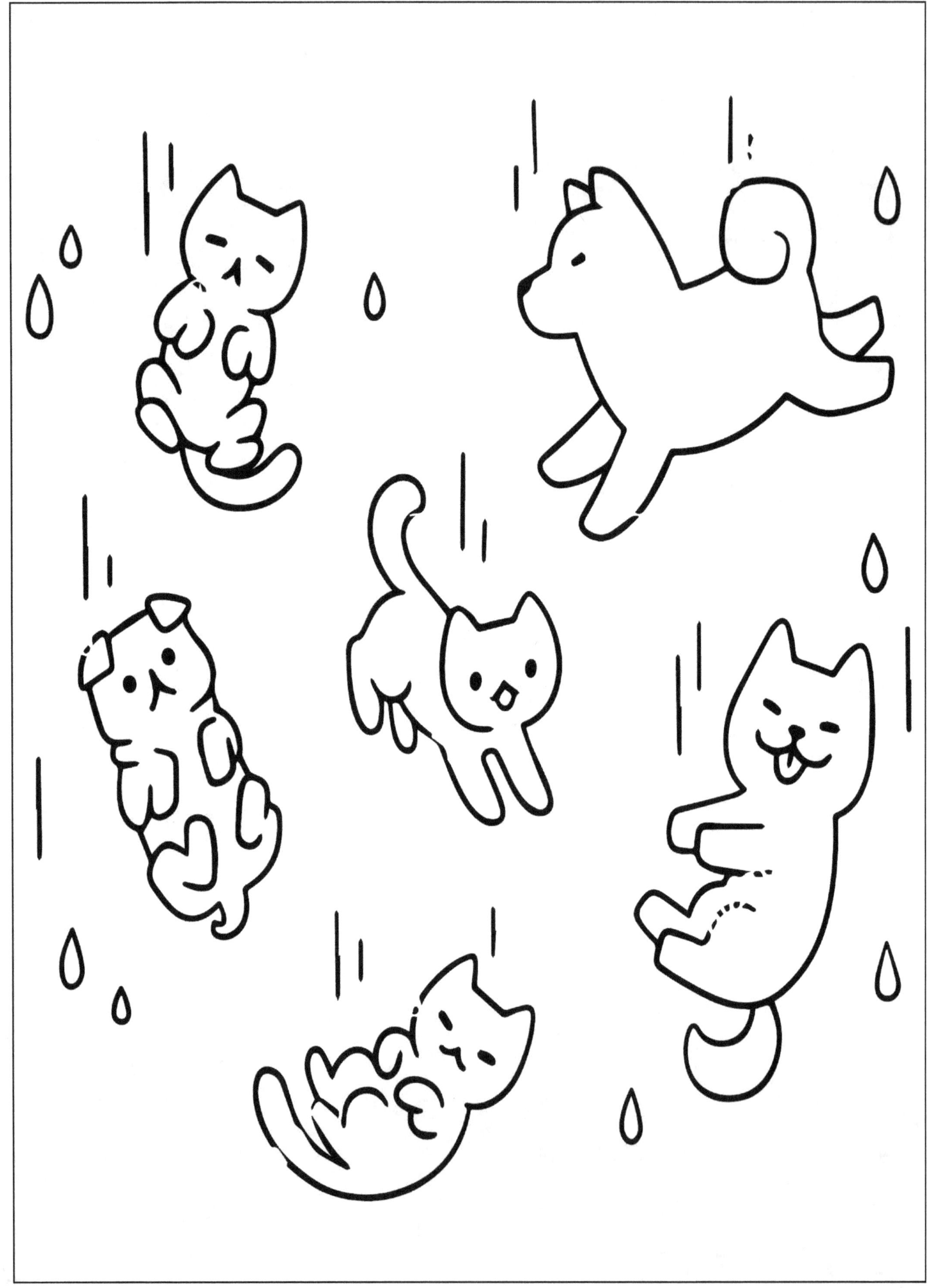

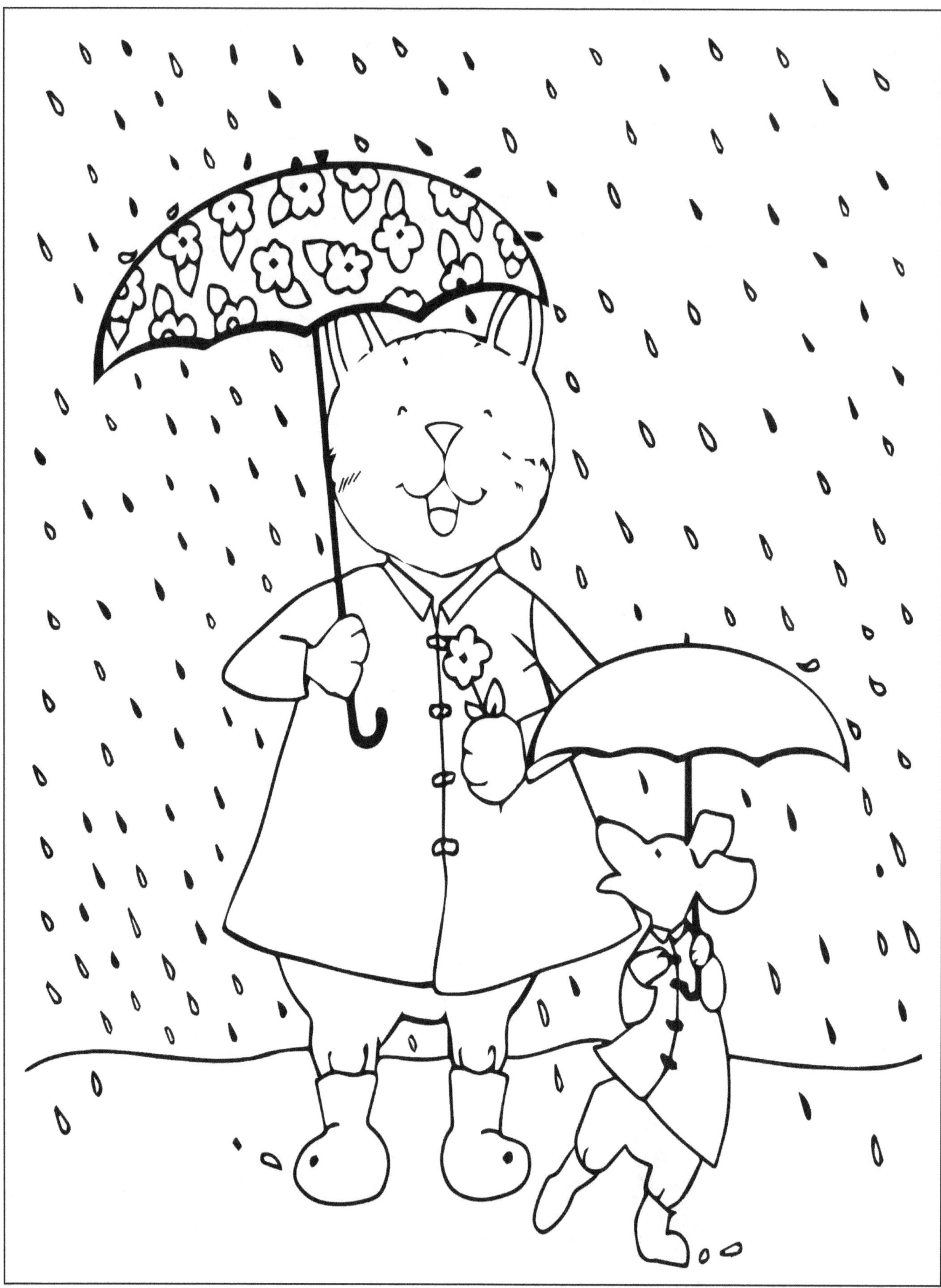

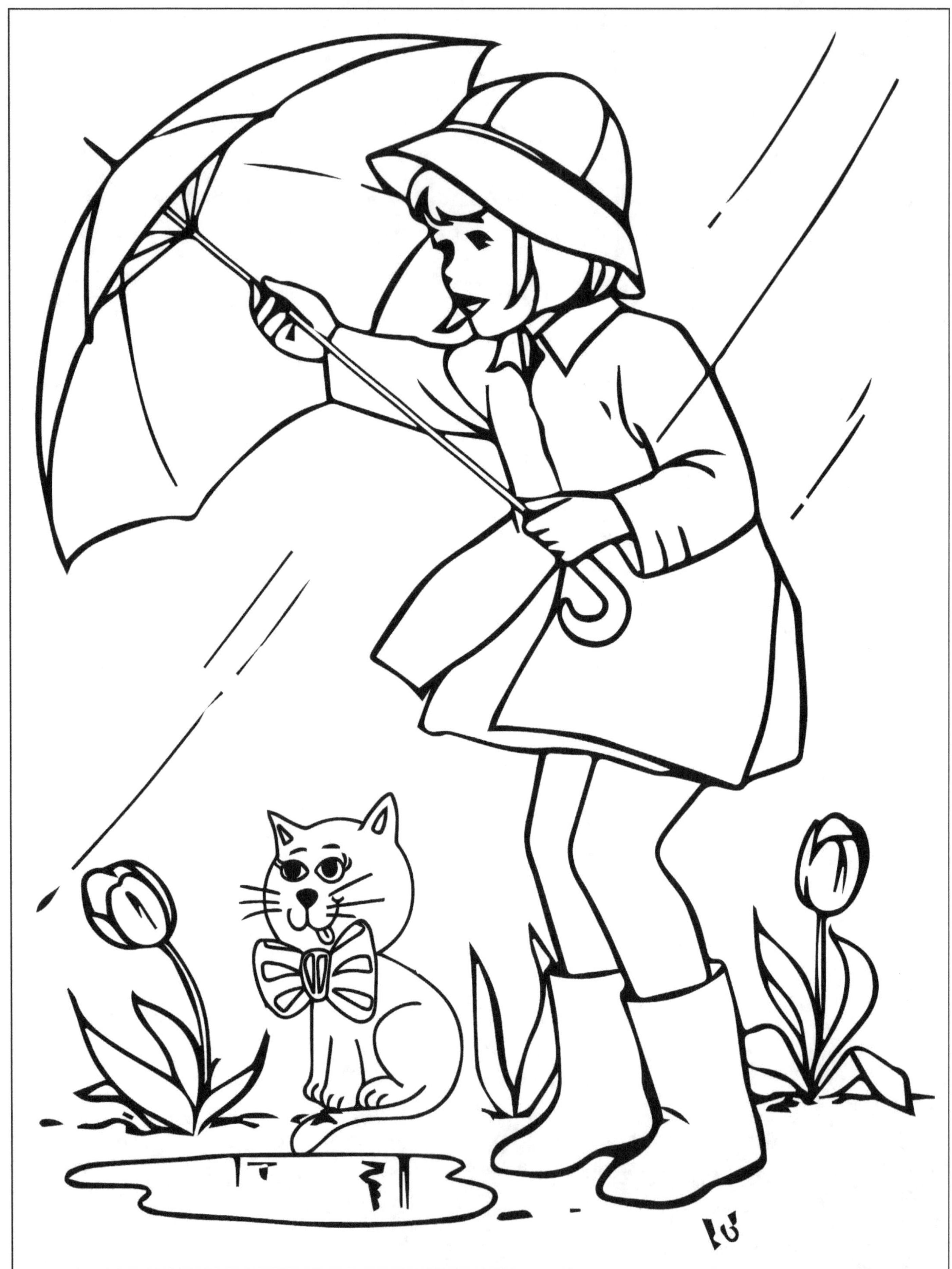

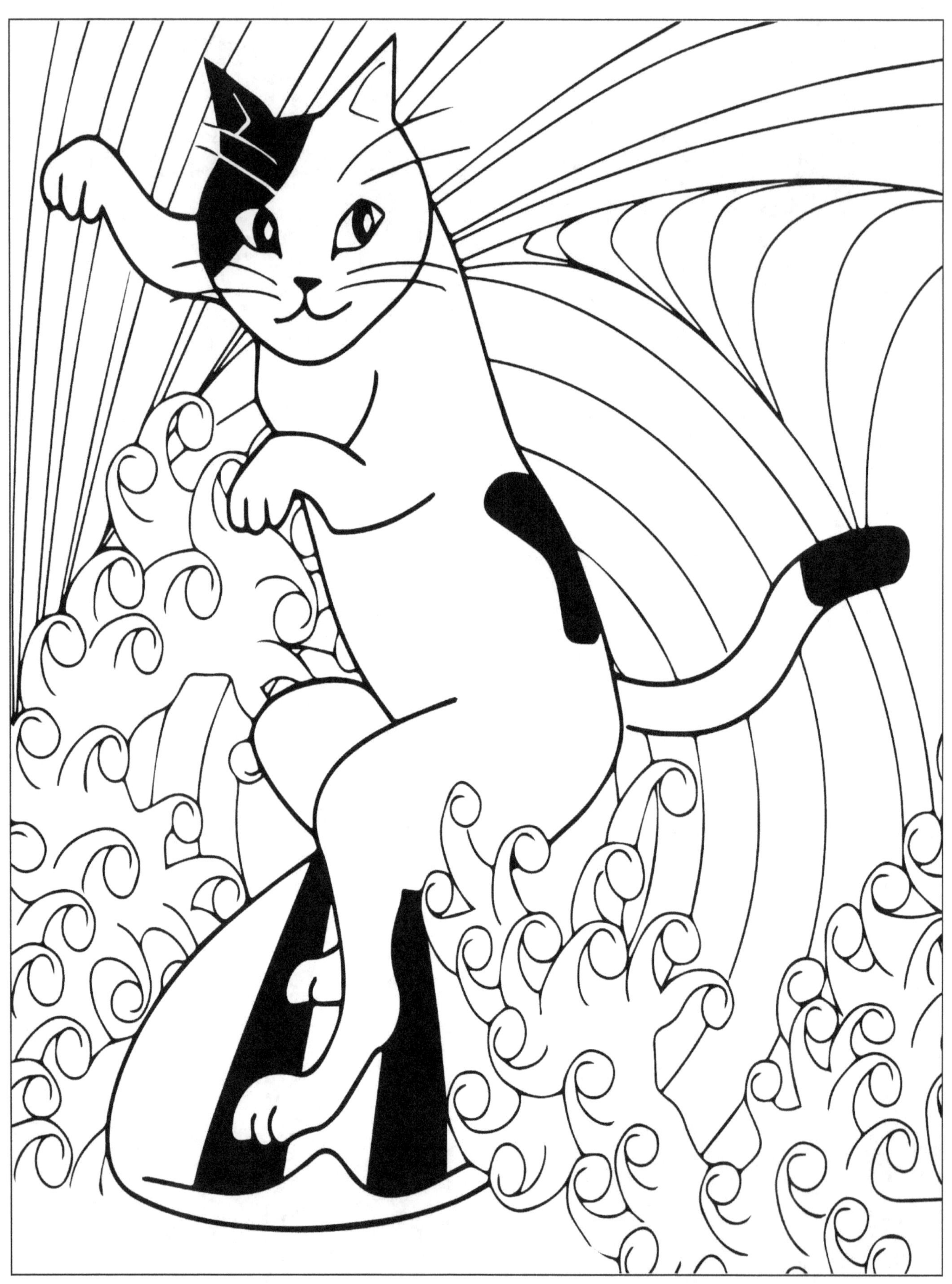

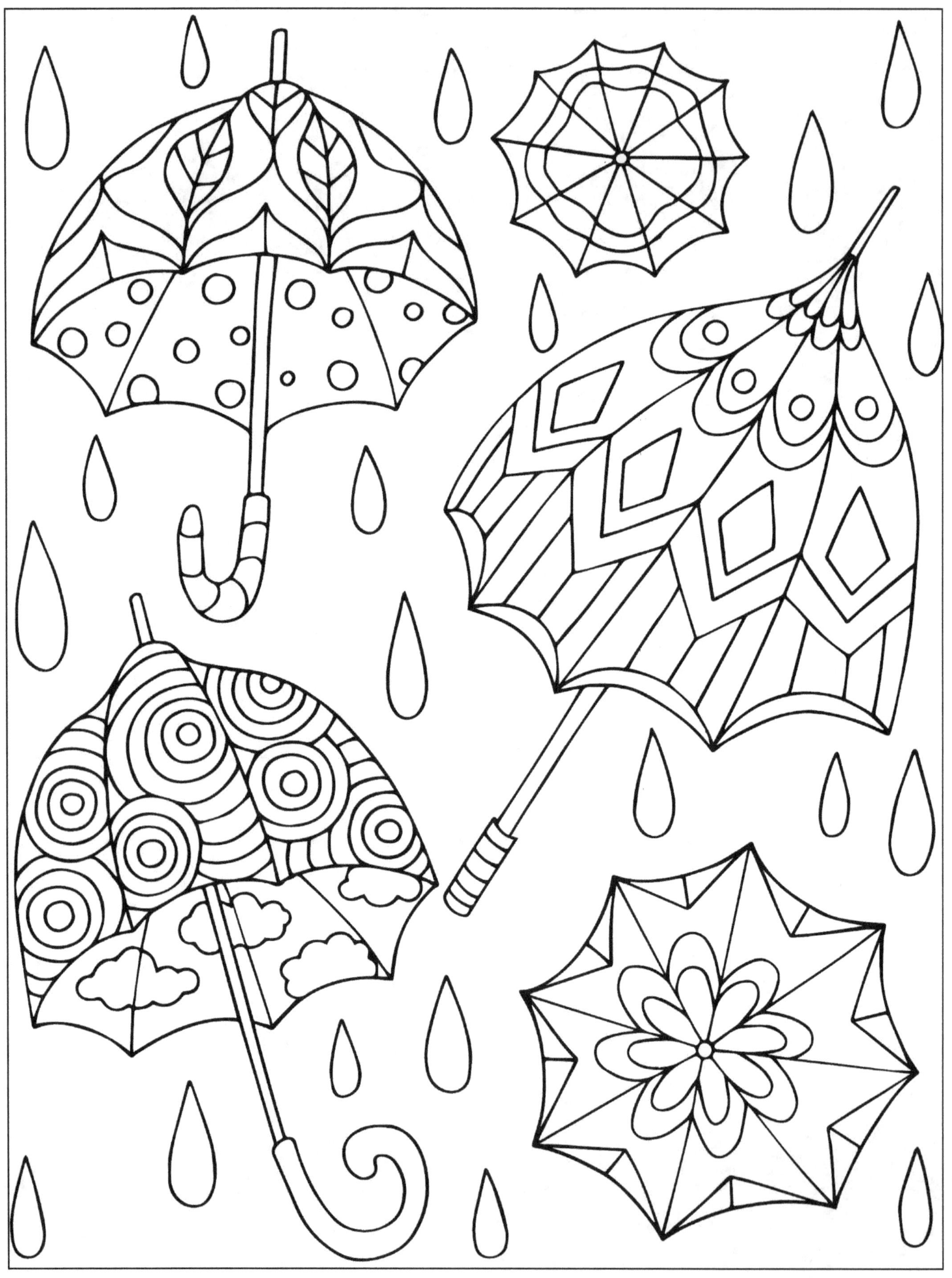

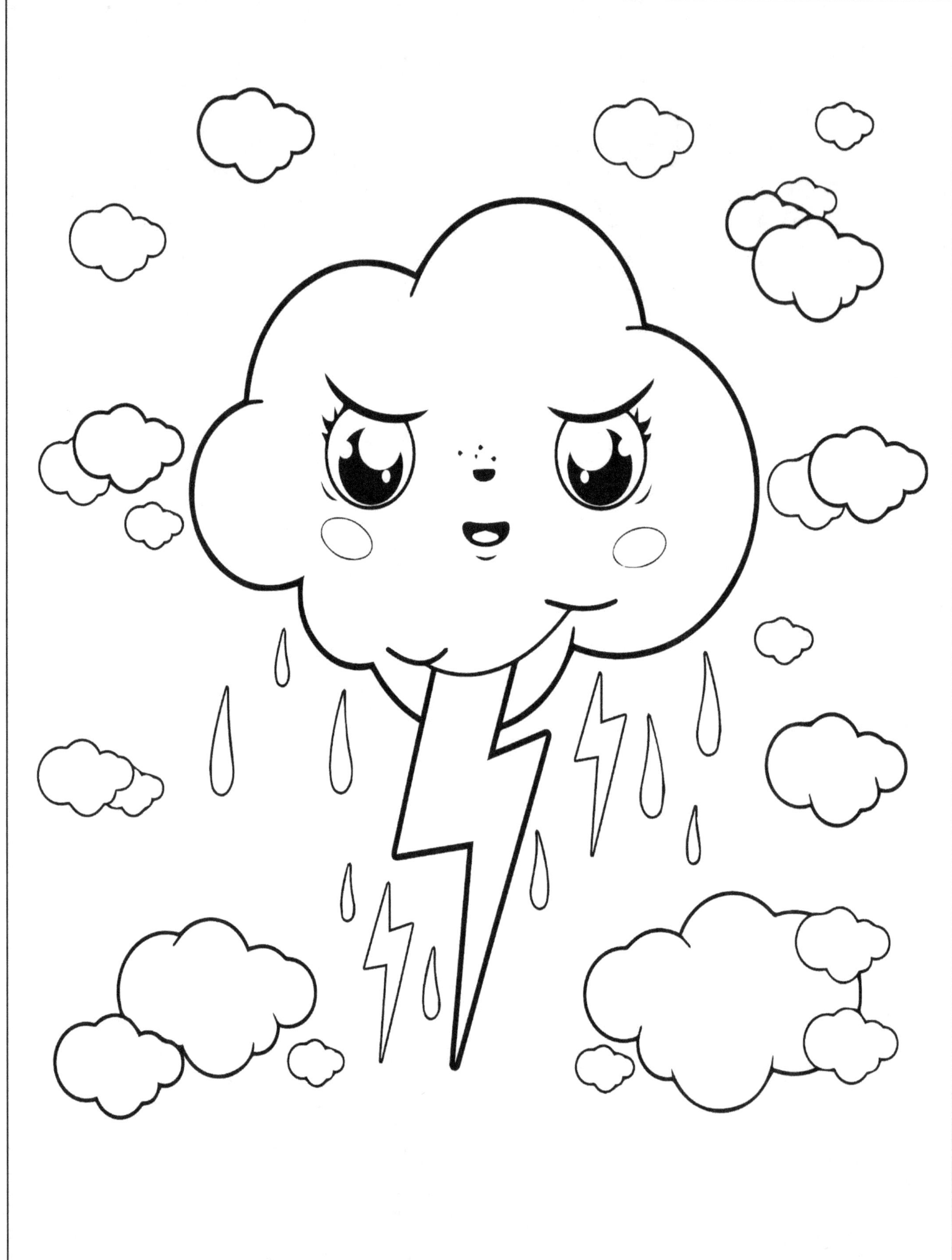

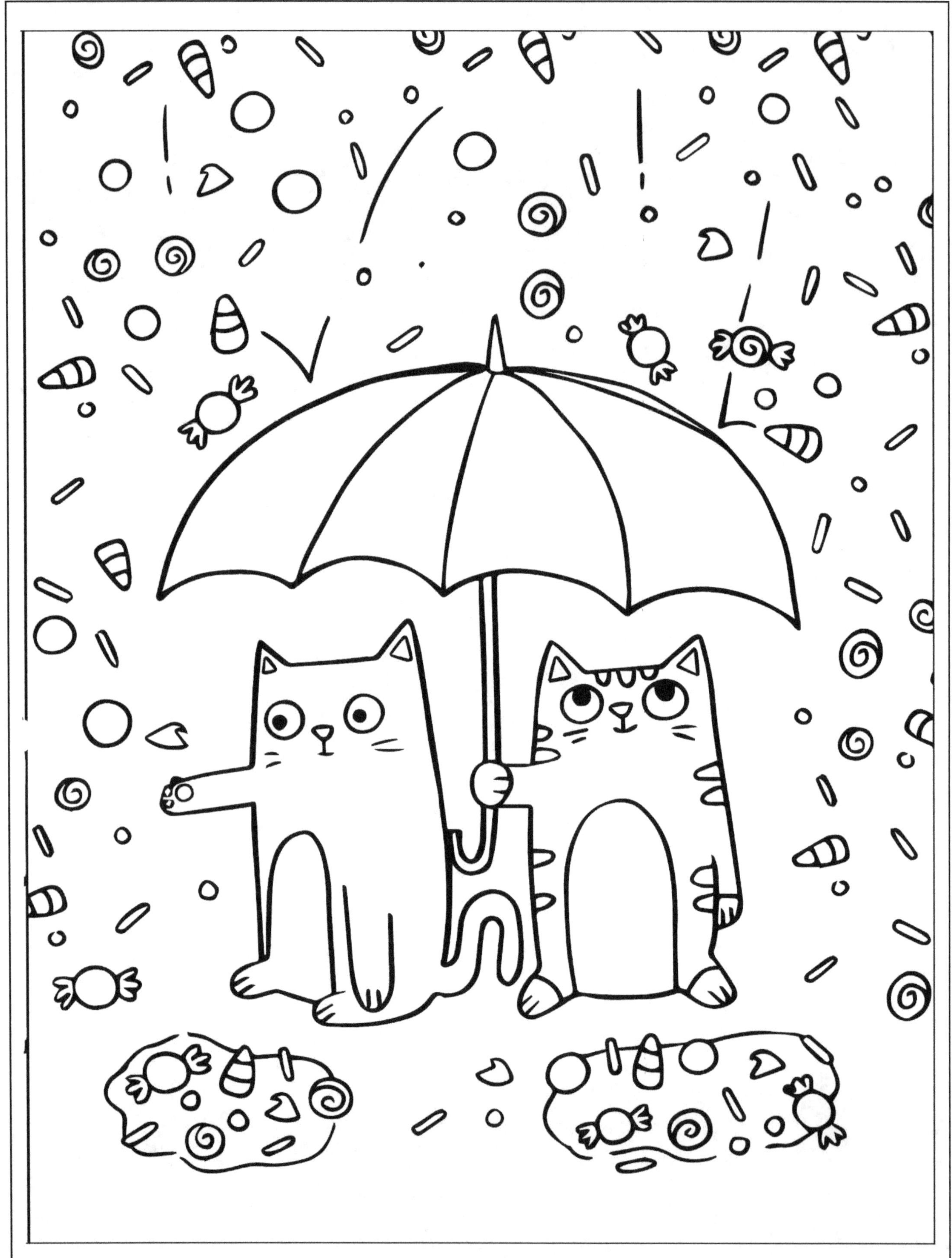

www.ingramcontent.com/pod-product-compliance
Lightning Source LLC
Chambersburg PA
CBHW081234250726
48654CB00012B/1325

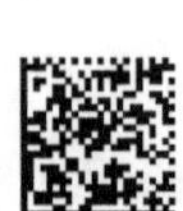